# These Englishmen Who Died for France

## Jean-Michel Steg

Foreword by John Horne

Translated by Ethan Rudell

UNIVERSITY OF **BUCKINGHAM** PRESS

Published by University of Buckingham Press,
an imprint of Legend Times Group
51 Gower Street
London WC1E 6HJ
info@unibuckinghampress.com
www.unibuckinghampress.com

First published in French in 2016 by Éditions Fayard

© Jean-Michel Steg, 2016, 2022
Translation © Ethan Rudell, 2016

The right of the above author and translator to be identified as the author and
translator of this work has been asserted in accordance with the Copyright,
Designs and Patents Act 1988. British Library Cataloguing in Publication Data
available.

ISBN (paperback): 9781800310872
ISBN (ebook): 9781800310889

Cover design: Ditte Løkkegaard

*For Paul Feunette, in memoriam*

# CONTENTS

Happy are those who died for the carnal earth,
Provided that it was in a just war.
Happy are those who died for a patch of ground.
Happy are those who died a solemn death.

Charles Péguy, *Ève* (1913)

# FOREWORD

The Battle of the Somme lives on in the collective memory of Great Britain, Northern Ireland and the countries of the Commonwealth (Australia, Canada, New Zealand) as the most dramatic episode of the Great War. For it was at this moment that the mass armies entirely composed of volunteers levied in the conflict's first wave of enthusiasm encountered the industrial warfare of the Western Front. Baptism of fire and baptism of blood! The battle's first day – 1 July 1916 – remains notorious for the scale of human losses suffered by the British army, which were greater than on any other single day in its entire history. Many British citizens are familiar with the Battle of the Somme, particularly through the work of the war's most famous writers – Wilfred Owen, Edmund Blunden and Robert Graves. Lasting four and a half months, it is above all seen as a monument to the tragedy, if not the futility, of the war – of all wars.

A very different interpretation is advanced by the British school of military historians. They tend to see the battle as the beginning of a true 'learning curve' that would lead the

British army to play a prominent role in the victory in 1918. Yet the French are curiously unfamiliar with the Battle of the Somme, and this despite the substantial contribution of the French army, which suffered around 20 per cent of all losses. Overshadowed by the Battle of Verdun, to which it was nevertheless intimately related, the Battle of the Somme (like that of Verdun for the British) occupies a marginal place in French national memory. It is as if each nation only has room for 'its' symbolic battle.

For the Germans, the Somme was at the time seen as a challenge: to defend the Reich's outposts in enemy territory across the Rhine. While the battle continued to serve as a reference point in the interwar years, it was subsequently overshadowed by Verdun and the theme of Franco-German reconciliation. If the battlefields of the Somme are today a site of memory and pilgrimage, it is thus above all for the citizens of the United Kingdom and the former Dominions of the Commonwealth. More than ever, it is the accents of London, Glasgow, Toronto, Melbourne and many other distant cities that one hears in the cemeteries and taverns of Picardy, making it a little corner of the vast British world that existed at the time of the Great War.

This makes the present work – a clear and accessible presentation of the Battle of the Somme from the British point of view – all the more relevant. Without neglecting the soldiers' experiences, it offers well-grounded judgements regarding the nature of the battle, its place in the war and the role of the high command. It exhibits an excellent mastery of the strategic and tactical aspects of the battle's first day, and gives an idea of the dimensions of a struggle that was to continue until November 1916. It nicely situates Britain's role in the battle (its subject) relative to that of France and Germany, and in doing so offers a view of the start of the Somme campaign that is more comprehensive than most other English-language studies, preoccupied as they are with 'their' battle.

The present work will help readers understand the importance of this battle for the United Kingdom and its Dominions as well as the traces it has left in politics, culture and memory. In the wake of the centenary year, Jean-Michel Steg's book thus comes as a welcome addition. Thanks to it, readers will better grasp what was, after its fashion, the 'British Verdun' and more fully appreciate its status as the greatest battle of the conflict (at least in terms of casualties). Jean-Michel Steg has written a book that is as succinct as it is wise, one that goes straight to the heart of this terrible ordeal and the major place it continues to occupy, a century on, in the British world's memory of the Great War.

John Horne,
Emeritus Fellow of Trinity College, Dublin,
11 November 2021

# PREFACE

The centenary of the First World War has received frenzied coverage in the media. Is it any wonder? It is only now, a hundred years on, that the wounds left by this unprecedented trauma can be examined without provoking fresh pangs of memory, forcing one to rapidly halt the autopsy and cover everything in a protective and ultimately convenient shroud. As in the aftermath of the Shoah, the children of those who lived through this deeply traumatic experience were reluctant to question the taciturn survivors in their lifetimes.

It was only with their grandchildren and those who followed that it first became possible to reconstruct the hell through which their forefathers lived between 1914 and 1918.[1]

On a personal level, I spent several years immersed in studying the appalling casualties suffered by the French army at the very start of the hostilities. There is always something relevant to be learned, it seems to me, from studying the most extreme moments of a confrontation. This is particularly the case of spikes in mortality during the First World War, a conflict that was unprecedented in terms of its duration, extent and intensity. Such moments of extremity are not random statistical facts but rather result from the specific conjunction of major causes of death at a given time and place.

Those that came together, for example, on 22 August 1914. On this, the bloodiest day in French history, the tactics, organization and military culture that the French army had inherited from the eighteenth century collided head-on with the firepower of the enemy's early twentieth-century weapons. On this day alone, more than 27,000 French soldiers were to die.

In a similar paroxysm of violence, on 1 July 1916 nearly 20,000 British and Dominion soldiers died in the space of just a few hours over a twenty-kilometre front stretching between Bapaume and Péronne, north of the river Somme. More soldiers were killed on that day than on any other in the entire history of the British army.

What does this moment teach us?

I began to look into this question after having attempted, in an earlier book, similarly to understand the events and significance of 22 August 1914.[2] In carrying out this work, I relied upon my own resources, those of a part-time student at Paris's École des Hautes Études en Sciences Sociales.

A belated part-time student but professional financier for more than thirty-five years, I was doubtless drawn to the subject of mass mortality partly because its study called upon some of my professional skills. It involved an effort to assign meaning to long series of numbers: how many dead? When? Where? In what way? How were the dead distributed by service, rank and professional, geographical and social origin?

As my work advanced, however, it was with some dismay that I found myself confronted with a simple reality, one that, in my naivety as a novice historian, I had not anticipated. Under the statistics of those killed were flesh-and-blood individuals. They are – or rather were – sons, brothers, husbands, fiancés and sometimes fathers. At a century's distance, it seems to me, reading their accounts and those of their friends and family produces a sort of cumulative effect, resonating all the more deeply as one's perception of the facts grows more detailed. Like the individual grains of a photograph – a metaphor that, rightly or wrongly, imposes itself upon the reader – each of them contributes to bringing their fate into ever sharper focus. In this way, a purely historical study of the facts is gradually supplemented by emotion and then memory.

For the purposes of my study and, later, as part of various projects, colloquia and commemorative programmes, I made multiple trips to a number of battlefields where, in the war's first weeks, what was known as the 'Battle of the Frontiers' took place. On several occasions, in particular, I visited the battlefields surrounding the village of Rossignol, in the Belgian Ardennes. There, on 22 August 1914, French troops saw horribly bloody combat. The scenery there is in general rural and serene, especially in summertime. Though intense, the fighting there was short-lived, with the front immediately shifting to the south. In contrast to some zones of north-eastern France, the area was thus not devastated by months and sometimes years of shelling and combat. On each visit, however, I was struck by how small these sites of mass death really are. To read regimental reports and survivors' accounts is to imagine vast expanses. Once there, however, one finds oneself looking across fields and pastures no larger than a couple of football pitches. Instinctively and with sudden horror, one imagines the soldiers of the time moving forward amid the bodies of their already dead and wounded comrades. To this horror is added incomprehension: faced with the firepower of modern weapons, how could they hope to cross dozens of metres of exposed terrain? And yet they threw themselves into the assault, sometimes several times over.

I felt this same horror mixed with incomprehension the first time I visited the sites of the Battle of the Somme near Beaumont-Hamel. There, on 1 July 1916, hundreds of Newfoundland Regiment volunteers hurled themselves into an assault against

German trenches located at the foot of a little hill held by British troops. By descending the side of the hill on foot, one's eyes fixed on the curtain of trees where the German trenches were located less than two hundred metres below, one cannot help but feel a disagreeable feeling of quasi-nudity. There is no natural obstacle behind which to hide, even if one were to throw oneself to the ground, and the awareness dawns on one that one's silhouette would have been perfectly outlined on the horizon for the defenders located on the opposite slope. In such circumstances, it would have been impossible, one tells oneself, to cross more than a few dozen metres under machine-gun fire. And this was indeed the case on that July morning.

Memory joins emotion by virtue of the fact that trips to the battlefields of the First World War nearly always include visits to the cemeteries that line them. Whereas the former are striking in point of their small size, the latter impress by their extent and (apparent) uniformity. Those who died on 22 August 1914, like those who died on 1 July 1916, are gathered together in cemeteries in which each gravestone bears a different name and distinct date of birth, but a single, uniform date of death. Whether at the Orée du Bois ('Wood's Edge') cemetery in Rossignol, where the young French volunteers of the Colonial Corps lie,[3] or that of Beaumont-Hamel, the last resting place of the Scottish and Newfoundlander[4] volunteers of the Somme, it is the same, seeping sadness. Yet there is a fundamental difference between the two sites. One is almost completely absent from French collective memory; the other is essential to the way in which the British remember and commemorate the First World War.

In October 2013, I published a book revisiting the battles of August 1914 and, in particular, that of Rossignol. I was subsequently approached by the descendants of some of those who fought there that day. Some of them wished to supply (useful and necessary) information. Others were simply glad to discuss these terrible events – important components of their family history that, in contrast to the battles of the Marne, Verdun and Chemin des Dames, generally receive so little attention. Given the calendar and the forthcoming commemorations of the Great War, we agreed to meet up for the anniversary of the Battle of Rossignol. We soon realized, however, that in the legitimate avalanche of commemorations that began in summer 2014, nothing – absolutely nothing – had been done by anyone for the anniversary of the war's bloodiest engagement, a day that was also the deadliest in all of French history. Thus, on 22 August 2014, a number of us – descendants of combatants with a keen interest in the war or people merely curious to know more – privately met at Rossignol to lay a few flowers and observe a moment of silence before the humble monument to the soldiers of the French Colonial Corps.

As I have had several opportunities to note, by contrast, it is impossible to travel the roads of the front line of the Somme between Bapaume and Péronne without encountering, whatever the time of year, a large number of anglophone visitors. Indeed, one need only glance at the bilingual window fronts of the local taverns and bars to form an idea of the important place that the Battle of the Somme occupies in the memory of the various parts of the British world.* The English, Scottish, Irish, Welsh, Orangemen of Ulster, Canadians, New Zealanders and even Bermudians (whose fate was particularly tragic on 1 July 1916)… each of the peoples of the United Kingdom and the Commonwealth actively recall the memory of their forefathers who (voluntarily, one must always remind oneself) came to Picardy to fight and die in 1916. Stelae, monuments, plaques and little museums recalling these various groups are everywhere to be found. At 7.30 in the morning every 1 July, thousands of visitors line up along the various stretches of the battlefield to sing 'God Save the Queen'. Despite the apparent similarity of these episodes, the national collective memories of

---

* The word 'Englishmen' in the title is a translation of the French 'Anglais', and is simply a colloquial shorthand for English-speakers from all the nations of the United Kingdom, as well as from its Dominions.

France and Britain operate in very different ways. The reason for this difference between neighbours and allies is an enigma that has dogged me since I began studying these questions. I must admit that I have been unable to find a single, fully satisfying explanation. Having lived in Great Britain for the past several years, I have been struck by the manner in which the British and French respectively recall and commemorate the First World War and its various episodes. Throughout 2016, discussions in the British media regarding the war's onset thus focused on the role each party played in the outbreak of the conflict: who was responsible? Could the catastrophe have been avoided if one leader or another had behaved differently? These questions, it seemed to me, were only very occasionally raised in France. From the French point of view, things are simple: the war broke out when Germany decided to invade France and Belgium. Protected by their island status and the Royal Navy, the British could have chosen to stay out of the conflict. They did not do so.

This is a crucial fact in itself, a dramatic departure from the United Kingdom's historical attitude vis-à-vis Continental Europe, the consequences of which may still be felt a hundred years later in the intense political debates regarding the country's place in Europe.

Admittedly, the violation of Belgian neutrality – since 1830 guaranteed by Great Britain, France and Germany – constituted a major problem for Europe's oldest constitutional state.[5] It is also true that, since the restoration of the German Empire in 1871, political, economic, colonial and military (and particularly naval) rivalry with the Second Reich had only increased. It was far from obvious, however, that Britain would come to France's aid, their recent and very informal Entente Cordiale notwithstanding. Over the course of the preceding millennium, Britain had suffered only one large-scale invasion – in 1066, from the Norman coast. In 1914, the French army and navy could still be seen as the essential hereditary enemy. Neither the joint expedition in the Crimea against the Russians in 1854 nor the happy years spent by the future Edward VII in Parisian salons of all types at the turn of the century had sufficed to erase this centuries-old Franco-British rivalry, which was often marked by open conflict. Twenty-six years later, in what was to become his most famous speech, Marshal Pétain thus sought to justify his submission to Nazi Germany as follows: 'Frenchmen, you have a short memory...'[6]

Reflected in the immediate dispatch of the British Expeditionary Force to France in mid-August 1914, this dramatic change in relations between the French and British entered a new phase with the Battle of the Somme, which started on 1 July 1916.

On that day, a series of exceptional events came together: a major offensive was for the most part carried out by a British mass army rather than a contingent of professional soldiers (even if, at this stage, all were volunteers rather than conscripts). This offensive was not merely coordinated with the French army but rather conducted jointly with it. The decision to launch it had been taken in the course of an Allied conference held in the French town of Chantilly in December 1915. Its aim was to achieve a decisive breakthrough into the German lines, an objective that had not been reached in 1915. With the onset of the German offensive against Verdun in February 1916, relieving its French ally, now under strong pressure from the Germans, also became a priority of Britain's war effort.

Finally, the battle's first day was also to be the bloodiest in British military history. It is without historic precedent and (fortunately) remains unparalleled in terms of lethality.

It was the exceptional nature of the Battle of the Somme for British and French alike that caught my attention. I attempted to analyse it by recalling the facts but also by considering the major differences between the British and French memories of this same event.

There is a very English type of black humour to be found in the fact that the British army should have experienced the single bloodiest day in its history after launching an offensive partly designed to relieve a French army that had reached the point of exhaustion outside Verdun. France displayed relatively little gratitude for this sacrifice at the time and little has changed since then. In French memory, the heroic image of Verdun has eclipsed the other battles of the period. The absence of British bitterness – in the immediate post-war years as today – is all the more remarkable for that reason.

Although the meaning of the offensive remains ambiguous, the factual work of the contemporary historian is facilitated by an abundant bibliography on the subject, mainly in English. With regard to the archives, the usual military sources are complemented by a broad array of fascinating museum resources. In this connection, I would particularly like to mention the recently renovated Imperial War Museum in London and the outstanding Historial de Péronne, with its centre for historical research. Recommending that one visit both of these institutions does not relieve my debt towards them for the assistance they supplied. But it does allow me to steer those fascinated by the subject towards rich and enlightening encounters.

# INTRODUCTION

## THE BLOODIEST DAY IN BRITISH HISTORY

On 1 July 1916, at 7.30 in the morning, twenty-six divisions of the British army launched an attack on German trenches along a twenty-five-kilometre front north of the river Somme and extending from the villages of Gommecourt (to the north) and Montauban-de-Picardie (to the south).

Their attack was preceded by a preliminary artillery bombardment, the duration (eight days) and intensity (more than 1.7 million shells fired by 1,400 guns massed behind the front line) of which was without precedent in the conflict. At the day's end, nearly 60,000 British soldiers had been put out of action, including more than 20,000 dead. The majority were killed in the first minutes of the attack. Many others lay dying for hours in the 'no man's land' that stretched for a few hundred metres between the positions of the two armies.

At the same time, eight divisions of the French Sixth and Tenth armies attacked towards the town of Péronne. Although the French troops initially enjoyed some success, the day was to end in strategic failure for them as well. Yet French casualties in the battle's first day were significantly lower than those of their British allies, even when one takes into consideration the fact that the French force consisted of only one fifth as many troops.

In throwing themselves into battle, these men had a specific mission: to take successive control of the Germans' first two lines and thereby create the possibility for a breakthrough by two divisions of cavalry waiting since dawn a few kilometres to the rear. Upon receiving the order, these cavalrymen were literally to advance swords drawn.

By nightfall, almost no British soldiers had reached the other side's front line alive. In the rare cases where the attackers had here and there succeeded in taking control of a German trench, the survivors were immediately confronted with violent enemy bombardment followed by massive counter-attack. Exhausted and inadequately resupplied in human and material resources, they were in most cases killed, taken prisoner or forced to withdraw to positions that had been conquered with much difficulty just a few hours earlier. In both tactical and human terms, it was – and remains – the most catastrophic single day in all of British military history.


What was the context in which this offensive was conceived? What took place on the ground that day? What factors contributed to such a human catastrophe?

Did any of the parties make mistakes that could have – and should have – been avoided?

With a century's hindsight, it is possible to offer something of a response to these questions. In attempting to do so, it will be particularly helpful to start by reconstructing – literally at ground level – the experience of the men who threw themselves into the attack on that day.

# CHAPTER 1

## THE ANNIHILATION OF THE NEWFOUNDLAND REGIMENT

### 1 JULY 1916: 8.45 A.M. OUTSIDE BEAUMONT-HAMEL (SOMME)

Crouching in reserve trenches 250 metres behind the British front line (itself 300 metres from the Germans' advance trenches), the 800 men of the Newfoundland volunteer regiment had been waiting since dawn outside the ruins of the village of Beaumont-Hamel for the order to attack.

Up since dawn the previous day, the men arrived at their position before sunrise. The bombardment of the German lines had been under way for a week and was still in full swing. At 7.30 a.m. – that is, ten minutes before the time set for the start of the Allied assault – they were shaken by an explosion at what was known as Hawthorn Ridge, where over the preceding weeks British sappers had deposited eighteen tons of explosives in a mine dug under the north-west extremity of the German position.

Ten minutes later, the Irish soldiers of the 1st Royal Inniskilling

Fusiliers and their Welsh counterparts from the 2nd South Wales Borderers left their front-line trenches at their officers' whistle to attack the German positions, which were located slightly downhill from them at a distance of roughly 300 metres. Having been alerted by the mine's explosion, however, the German defenders rapidly left their deep concrete shelters and were already at firing positions that had been prepared in advance.

Natives of Baden-Württemberg, the German soldiers of the 119th Reserve Regiment of the 29th Infantry Division had been stationed at this position for nearly twenty months. In contrast to the Allies, the German army only rarely rotated its troops from one part of the front to another. It was they who, in this relatively calm sector since the front became bogged down in the autumn of 1914, dug the deep concrete shelters that (mainly) protected them from the unremitting fire of British artillery. Above all, they had had the opportunity to reconnoitre each bit of no man's land and establish precise firing coordinates for their machine-gun nests and trench artillery positions. It was also at this time that the German artillery, which had for a week been nearly silent in order to avoid giving away its specific location to the British, went into action behind the lines. Like their counterparts in the trenches, German gunners had long ago collected the firing coordinates that would allow them to concentrate their fire on no man's land, the British departure trenches and the communication trenches that permitted supplies and reinforcements to be transported to the front.

As everywhere else on this day, the initial bombardment failed to destroy the Germans' ability to defend their first line. Exposed in their slow advance over the bare soil of no man's land as they made their way under shellfire between craters and masses of barbed wire, the attackers were annihilated by enemy fire.

Thirty minutes later, a second assault wave, consisting of the troops of the King's Own Scottish Borderers, was launched. It met the same fate. Indeed, as anticipated by the plan of attack, the British battery fire had by then progressed beyond the German front lines. Decided in advance, the firing programme was based on the assumption that British troops would have already taken control of them by this time. In addition to protecting the soldiers from possible German counter-attack, it was also necessary to prevent them from falling victim to friendly fire. Some of the troops carried a large metal triangle on the back of their uniforms, which was supposed to help reconnaissance aircraft monitor their progress as they flew over the battlefield. Relieved that the bombardment had finally come to an end but filled with rage after having been subjected to it non-stop for a week, many German soldiers left their trenches and sat right down on the parapets. From there, they fired at the British soldiers as they left their starting trenches, their silhouettes outlined against the horizon like targets at a fairground shooting gallery. Insufficiently damaged by the bombardment, the barbed-wire entanglements once again slowed the British advance. Where British pioneer troops had succeeded in cutting a path, German machine guns, with an unobstructed view of the battlefield, were able to concentrate their fire precisely.

As often on that day, the information received at British 29th Division headquarters, whose two brigades (the 86th and 88th) had been tasked with rapidly taking Beaumont-Hamel, was confusing and contradictory. Messages arrived indicating very heavy losses but some believed that Scottish units had succeeded in reaching the German lines. A white flare had even been seen, though it was unclear which side had fired it. Its meaning was thus not clear: was it a sign from the Scots that the German trench had been occupied or rather a request from the German defenders for their artillery to lengthen their fire?

The commander of the 29th Division, General de Beauvoir de Lisle, thus decided to send in the two regiments of the

88th Brigade, which had been held in reserve to supply the third wave of assault. They consisted of the 1st Essex and 1st Newfoundland – the regiment of Newfoundland volunteers.

## NEWFOUNDLAND IN 1914

Many of the British soldiers who fought that day were drawn from the enthusiastic but inexperienced volunteer units that had enlisted in the first days of August 1914. The Newfoundlander soldiers had for their part already seen battle in the course of the conflict.

A large island off the north-eastern coast of Canada that had long been a British colony, Newfoundland was a fully fledged Dominion when the war broke out, a status it had acquired in 1907 (like New Zealand the same year). It was thus by an independent parliament that the decision was taken to send, at the territory's cost, a regiment of volunteers to fight for the motherland within the British army.

At the time, the population of Newfoundland was just more than 240,000 people. It had neither a standing army nor even a militia, much less conscription. Its capital, St John's, possessed three scouting troops (organized by their respective churches: the Anglican, Catholic and Methodist) and a shooting club. It had been a long time since Newfoundlanders had last fought the Native Americans or their traditional adversary, the French. Scoured by the winds of the North Atlantic, life was harsh on the island and its society was relatively divided: on the one hand, there were those who lived from cod fishing and the activities with which it was associated; on the other, there were the miners, trappers and tradesmen who supplied the remainder of the population. The social separation between Anglicans (of English origin), Catholics (of Irish origin), Presbyterians (of Scottish origin) and Methodists (of English or Welsh origin) was also quite real. Yet the fervour to enlist in defence of Great Britain was massive and general. The large number of volunteers who presented themselves had no barracks to house them, no uniforms to wear and no weapons with which to equip themselves. They were gathered together on a St John's cricket field in tents made of sailcloth that had been donated by the merchant ships stationed in the port; their uniforms were made of blue cloth (the only available locally) rather than khaki. They had no weapons apart from those available at the shooting club and whatever hunting rifles they possessed. Above all, there was no one to supply them with even the most basic military instruction. Ultimately, an old soldier was found in the capital who had retired after twenty-five years of service in the British army. He immediately received the regiment's first officer's brevet. For the first two months, the better part of their training consisted in marching in columns around the cricket field. The rifles ordered from Canada only arrived after the first contingent of volunteers had shipped out.

For on 4 October, 500 of them had embarked for England. They spent around ten months training in England and then Scotland, this time in more structured fashion, with the group periodically receiving new volunteers from Newfoundland. In February 1915, the 1st Regiment of Newfoundland volunteers was thus officially formed with more than a thousand men.

On 19 September 1915, the regiment, now assigned to the British 29th Infantry Division, landed at Suvla Bay to play its part within the British Expeditionary Force at Gallipoli, located in European Turkey. It was there that the Newfoundlander soldiers had their baptism of fire, though they arrived too late to participate in major attacks. They nevertheless took a little promontory by storm, naming it Caribou Hill after the symbol of their territory. They also familiarized themselves with the discomfort and disastrous sanitary conditions of trench life, made worse by the climate. Finally, they were exposed to Turkish sniper fire and artillery bombardment. After having lost around sixty men, half of them from illness (dysentery and so on), the Newfoundlander soldiers were among the last to re-embark on 9 January 1916, doing so under enemy fire. Until 1 July, they held relatively calm positions but were engaged in sustained patrolling activity and raids against enemy positions.

## THE ASSAULT

At 8.45 in the morning on 1 July, the commanders of the 29th Division's two reserve regiments (Essex and Newfoundland) thus independently received the order to attack.

After instructions had been transmitted to each company, the men of the 1st Newfoundland began to advance at 9.15. In front of them, the communication trenches leading to the British first-line and departure trenches had been completely disorganized by the German bombardment, a situation made worse by the ceaseless flow of Irish and Welsh wounded from the first two assault waves as they made their way back on foot or with the aid of stretcher-bearers. The Newfoundland Regiment could thus advance only very slowly along the obstructed, 1.5-metre wide communication trenches.

The regiment's commander, Lieutenant Colonel Arthur Lovell Hadow, an ambitious Englishman, then took a surprising decision, one that was to have major consequences: he ordered the troops to leave the communication trenches and, from the British second line, set off towards the German lines in assault formation over open ground. He thus forced the soldiers to cover twice as much open ground under enemy fire than planned.

The Newfoundlanders thus began to advance without cover according to the attack formation they had practised in training: two platoon lines separated by fifty paces. The bombardment slowed their progress, as did the fact that the men had to begin by extricating themselves from the British barbed wire meant to prevent a possible German attack. Since the soldiers were originally to have departed from their forward positions, the wire had not been cut before the attack. The backpacks they carried weighed more than thirty kilograms and contained a large amount of ammunition and all of the supplies needed for a full day of fighting. Before they even reached the British front line, which was supposed to have been their starting position, they had already sustained significant losses. But the Newfoundlander soldiers continued to advance while attempting to hold their lines; according to one witness, their chins were tucked in as if they were moving forward under a blizzard.

Those who reached what were supposed to have been their departure trenches, which slightly overlooked the German positions, were now in the direct line of sight of the Württemberger soldiers, their silhouettes clearly outlined against the horizon on this brilliant July morning. With the 1st Essex still moving slowly up the communication trenches, moreover, they were at this precise moment the only British soldiers on the move along this portion of the battlefield. All of the local German artillery thus concentrated its fire on the Newfoundlander soldiers. Most of the men did not even reach what were supposed to have been their departure trenches. Those who succeeded in moving beyond them got no further than what was known as 'Danger Tree', a petrified tree a few dozen metres on.[7]

The regiment's journal entry for 1 July summarized the situation with sobriety and honesty:

The enemy's fire was effective from the outset, but the heaviest casualties occurred on passing through the gaps in our front wire, where the men were mown down in heaps. Many more gaps in the wire were required than had been cut. In spite of losses the survivors steadily advanced until close to the enemies [sic] wire by which time very few remained. A few men are believed to have actually succeeded in throwing bombs into the enemy's trench.[8]

In fact, twenty minutes after having left their reserve trench (which they had named St John's Road), 85 per cent of the Newfoundland soldiers who had participated in the attack were dead, dying or wounded. This was the highest rate of casualties of any British unit that fought that day. At 9.45, from his shelter Lieutenant Colonel Lovell Hadow informed his hierarchical superior, the commander of the 88th Brigade, that the assault had failed. He then received the order to collect the survivors and send them back into battle, an order that he accepted. Yet a general-staff officer who had observed the massacre (from a distance) cancelled the order and suspended offensive operations in the sector for the remainder of the day. Throughout the afternoon and, above all, the evening, the wounded crawled back towards British lines. The last of them to reach the British lines did so on 5 July.

Nearly 800 men and officers directly participated in the attack. The next morning, only sixty-eight of them answered the regiment's call. All of the others were dead, wounded or missing. There were no longer any able-bodied officers. Among the 347 dead and wounded were four sets of brothers. It seems that not a single German soldier was killed in the Newfoundlanders' assault. It was only four months later – on 13 November 1916 – that a regiment of Scottish Highlanders would finally succeed in taking what had been the first wave's objective when it set out that 1 July morning at 7.30: the German trench line 300 metres distant.

# CHAPTER 2

## WHY A FRANCO-BRITISH OFFENSIVE ON THE SOMME IN THE SUMMER OF 1916?

### GENESIS OF THE OFFENSIVE

In early December 1915, French and British general staff and political leaders held a joint conference in Chantilly to review the war's progress. At this conference, they decided to launch what they hoped would be a decisive offensive the following year.[9] Its objective was to take advantage of the British army's growing strength in France (a matter not just of troop numbers but also of improved training in modern combat methods). Together with the French army, the aim was to build a fighting force with enough firepower and troops to break the German defences. At the same time, the Russian army would launch a large offensive (what would become the Brusilov Offensive), and the Italian army, which had just entered the conflict on the Allied side, would for its part also go on the attack.

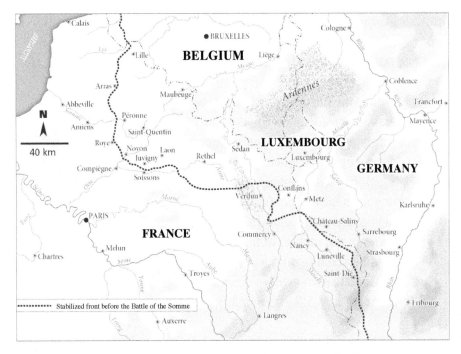

THE STABILIZED FRONT (LATE 1914-EARLY 1915)

Conceived by the French and British general staffs and approved by the respective war cabinets (led by Herbert Asquith and Aristide Briand), the idea of a joint offensive constituted a new and significant step in relations between the two countries and the conduct of the war. Although France and Great Britain had entered the war in August 1914 within twenty-four hours of one another, there was initially no reason to expect that their military operations would be jointly conducted. The instructions from the Secretary of State for War, Lord Kitchener, to the commander of the BEF,[10] the appropriately named Field Marshal John French, on 19 August 1914 are in this respect particularly enlightening:

It must be recognized from the outset that the numerical

strength of the British Force and its contingent reinforcement is strictly limited, and with this consideration kept steadily in view it will be obvious that the greatest care must be exercised towards a minimum of losses and wastage. Therefore, while every effort must be made to coincide most sympathetically with the plans and wishes of our Ally, the gravest consideration will devolve upon you as to participation in forward movements where large bodies of French troops are not engaged and where your Force may be unduly exposed to attack. Should a contingency of this sort be contemplated, I look to you to inform me fully and give me time to communicate to you any decision to which His Majesty's Government may come in the matter. In this connection I wish you distinctly to understand that your command is an entirely independent one, and that you will in no case come in any sense under the orders of any Allied General.[11]

Although there were contacts between soldiers from the start of the Entente Cordiale in 1908, the first weeks of the war illustrated how difficult it could be for the generals of the two armies to cooperate and even sometimes to communicate. The most striking example of this was the decision by General Lanrezac, commander of the French Fifth Army, to abandon abruptly his army's positions on the Sambre and Meuse on 23 August 1914, without bothering to inform the leaders of the BEF, which was covering its left flank. Suddenly finding themselves isolated vis-à-vis the German offensive, it was only the skilful marksmanship of the British soldiers before Mons that saved them from being overwhelmed, encircled and destroyed by the enemy.

It should be noted that historical examples of active cooperation between the British and French armies are as rare as cases of confrontation between them are frequent.[12] In late 1915, however, relations between Joseph Joffre, the French commander-in-chief, and his British counterpart,

Field Marshal Douglas Haig, who had just replaced French, were rather good. They thus settled upon the idea of jointly preparing and conducting an offensive. The site chosen was the Somme, where British units newly arrived from Great Britain and the Dominions gradually took over from French units. Many British military leaders would have preferred an offensive in the Pas-de-Calais: it was there that the BEF had mainly fought since autumn 1914 and it thus knew the terrain well. Given the proximity of the Channel ports, this also would have facilitated British logistics. On the Somme, by contrast, new depots would need to be constructed as well as new rail lines to supply them. But it was the Somme that constituted the junction point of the two armies that were to act in concert. In early February, confirmation was received that the offensive would indeed take place on the Somme before summer.

All of these plans were shattered by the German offensive at Verdun, which began on 21 February 1916. The German chief of staff, Erich von Falkenhayn, decided not to passively await the anticipated Allied offensive. Outside the fortified city of Verdun, the front followed a salient to the north. Its layout allowed the Germans to plan a three-sided attack to reduce it. Forcing the French to abandon Verdun would not necessarily provide the Germans with a decisive strategic breakthrough, but, at this stage in the war, the city's fall would come as a very heavy blow to the French war effort, at once sapping the country's military strength and its morale. This is precisely why the French general staff chose to maintain its positions on the right bank of the Meuse at all costs despite the violence of the attack. In a remark that post-dates the failure of the initial attack, Falkenhayn described this as an opportunity to 'bleed the French army white'. After the fact, the leaders of both sides doubtless sought to redescribe failed breakthrough offensives as operations to wear down the enemy. Thus Joffre's famous attempt at self-justification following the bloody offensives in Artois and Champagne, which had been intended to break open the front in 1915: 'I am gnawing away at them...'

The French general staff decided to hold on at all costs rather than to carry out a tactical withdrawal that, in military terms, would have been entirely conceivable. It henceforth concentrated all of its human and material resources on defending Verdun. This nearly superhuman effort immediately had very major consequences for the anticipated offensive on the Somme. On the one hand, it became urgent to launch an offensive that would, it was hoped, force the Germans to withdraw troops and materiel from the Verdun front. On the other hand, it was now clear that French and British forces could no longer devote equal resources and efforts to this offensive. The debate continued over the weeks that followed, with the French general staff lodging increasingly insistent appeals for an offensive while constantly reducing the human and material resources that it was ready to devote to it. Kitchener's position in Asquith's war cabinet was not sufficiently strong to oppose it.[13] As an experienced soldier, he wished to have as many well-trained troops as possible before launching a major offensive. Despite their very large numbers, however, the troops available to him in late 1915 were a disparate bunch, especially from a geographical point of view. In addition to forces from Great Britain (the English, of course, but also the Welsh and Scottish), 'Kitchener's Army' drew upon the broader United Kingdom (Ireland). Although Ireland had yet to win its independence, there was a genuine divide separating majority Catholic and nationalist southern counties from majority Protestant and loyalist northern counties, with many Irish units principally recruited on one side or the other of this still virtual frontier. Paradoxically, whether their recruitment was mainly Catholic or mainly Protestant, Irish units sought to rival one another on the battlefield, with Protestant troops seeking to underscore their intense patriotism while Catholic troops hoped once and for all to win Home Rule (in fact, independence). Next came the troops of the former white colonies, most of which had become Dominions independently governed under the entirely theoretical authority of the British sovereign. Such was the case of Australia, New Zealand, South Africa, Canada and Newfoundland. The volunteer soldiers from these territories were of European origin and often second- or even first-generation immigrants. Finally, there were contingents from the protectorates of Asia, which mainly consisted of Indian or Nepalese soldiers (the famous Gurkhas).

In this respect, the forthcoming battle on the Somme – like the jubilee of Queen Victoria several years earlier – was to be the high-water mark of a diverse and multinational 'imperial patriotism' distinctive to Britain.


At the same time, the objective assigned to the operation changed. Given the number of troops necessary to defend Verdun, the French army would play less of a role. Was it still possible to imagine a breakthrough battle, even along a smaller front? Should one not instead consider attacking along a broader front, above all to prompt the Germans to divert as many resources as possible from those presently concentrated on Verdun?

### THE BATTLE PLAN

The French and British military leaders tended to give ambiguous answers to clear questions. Even the British general staff never genuinely settled on the offensive's real strategic objective – far from it. The planned offensive thus contained contradictory elements. Some of them, such as the long preliminary bombardment and the choice of a relatively broad front, meant abandoning any hope of taking the enemy by surprise, making a breakthrough all the more difficult. Others, such as the decision to make several cavalry divisions available for the attack, suggested hopes for breakthrough. In mid-1916, however, none of the belligerents on the Western Front had succeeded in breaking through a front defended by deeply staggered lines of trenches. Since late 1914, when a continuous front running from the North Sea to the Vosges was first established, no side had succeeded in shifting it more than thirty kilometres in any direction. In the perpetual clash between offensive and defensive, sword and armour, a plateau had – for a short while – been reached. Entrenched behind a system of buried shelters, well prepared and in possession of unprecedented firepower, the defending side could block any infantry army, even a much larger one, from advancing.

To extricate itself from this strategic impasse, the British general staff sought a modern and industrial response: along the entire front of attack, the infantry's assault was to be preceded by a massive, continuous artillery bombardment. This was to be of such duration and intensity that it would destroy the enemy's defences before the infantry went into battle. Instead of rushing forward once the bombardment had ended, the infantry were to set off at a walk to occupy the enemy trenches. Their dazed defenders – those who had not already fled or been killed on the spot – would be waiting with their hands held high. Once the first line of trenches had been occupied, the artillery barrage would move on to the second-line and reserve trenches in order to allow the operation to be serially repeated until a breakthrough had been achieved or the enemy was so discouraged he sued for peace.

Such was the heart of the British battle plan on the Somme. It was to mark the shift to a genuine war of materiel. Henceforth, the advantage would no longer belong to the side capable of sending the largest number of foot soldiers into battle but rather to the nation that produced – or could abundantly procure – the most modern arms and ammunition. It was, in short, to be a war of materiel in which Great Britain might take full advantage of its industrial, commercial and financial power to produce, buy and import, with protection from the Royal Navy, the equipment needed for victory.

As we have seen, this is not how things were to go on 1 July 1916. On that day, several critical elements prevented the British plan from being successfully carried out. Over most of the twenty-four-kilometre front assigned to British forces, the soldiers who hauled themselves over the parapets of the departure trenches most often found themselves faced with still-living defenders who were well equipped and waiting at their fighting posts. They faced shelling from the Germans' nearly intact long-range artillery and generally had to advance over broken ground on which the very effective barbed-wire networks had often not been destroyed.

As always in such circumstances over the course of the First World War, the attackers were decimated. On the first day of battle, territorial gains were non-existent over most of the British front and minimal in those portions adjoining French positions. So what happened?

# CHAPTER 3

## THE STRATEGIC CONTEXT: TRENCH WARFARE

The trenches have famously come to symbolize the war of 1914–18: for nearly four years, millions of men faced off against one another in appalling conditions along two parallel and nearly continuous lines stretching from the North Sea to Switzerland. Yet the war that the general staffs of both sides had imagined and prepared for prior to 1914 was the absolute antithesis of trench warfare. Relying upon the Schlieffen Plan and the doctrine of 'all-out offensive', respectively, the Germans and French above all sought a war of movement based upon the rapid transfer of great masses of men in a quest for decisive victory. How did the stalemate of autumn 1914 come about?

### THE ORIGIN OF THE TRENCHES

Since the start of the modern era, digging trenches was part of the know-how of European armies. It was a siege-war tactic that allowed the besiegers to approach enemy fortifications without incurring too many losses. Continuous trench networks were first built in an effort to reduce casualties during the Russo-Japanese War (1904–5), the first twentieth-century war between armies possessing modern firepower. A large number of Westerners observed the war on the ground and took note of this innovation, concluding that ever more rapid and violent attacks would henceforth be necessary to avoid what they saw as a regrettable stalemate.[14]

In the first weeks of the war, German troops thus dashed across Belgium in an effort to encircle and destroy the French army. In what was to become the 'Battle of the Frontiers', a major setback for the Allies, the French troops who went to meet them in Belgium, Lorraine and the Ardennes in mid-August found themselves faced with unprecedented firepower. Under German fire, French soldiers sought what refuge they could – behind their backpacks, in the shelter of embankments and then in individually dug holes. These 'foxholes' were gradually linked up in order to restore tactical links between the combatants. The success of the Battle of the Marne in mid-September 1914 partly depended on these early trenches, from which French foot soldiers, for once in a mainly defensive position, decimated the German assault waves.

The Germans responded with pragmatism to the failure of the Schlieffen Plan and completely changed their strategy. The final victory against France would wait; the military effort now had to be concentrated against the Russians on the Eastern Front. German troops in the west withdrew to a line connecting the modest high points of northern and eastern France (Vimy Ridge, Les Éparges hill, the Chemin des Dames, Vieil Armand in the Vosges, and so on). There, German engineers dug trenches that permitted a minimum number of troops to wait deep within French territory and in relative security until Russia's defeat allowed offensive operations to be resumed in the west. From 1914 to 1918, the Germans only launched three major offensives in the west: those of 1914 (Ypres), 1916 (Verdun) and spring 1918, on which they staked everything.

Following the bloody failure of his frontal assaults against the German positions, Joffre very reluctantly agreed to allow his soldiers to protect themselves by digging in. This is because the entire French military ethos was based on aggression, the spirit of the offensive and the urgent need to avoid ceding another inch of national territory to the enemy and reconquer that which had been lost. In autumn 1914, mutual attempts to outflank one's adversary had failed and the front was now continuous. The troops mobilized in August were exhausted by the fighting and constant movement. They had also suffered appalling losses, with the war's first weeks the deadliest of the entire conflict. They needed to catch their breaths a little and, reluctantly, the general staffs acknowledged this. The modern firepower at their disposal, however, meant that the two armies could not remain facing one another in the open field, even in the absence of a major offensive. Everywhere, they had to take refuge and dig in. Each side thus set about digging its own shelters in keeping with the layout and composition of the terrain as well as the units stationed there. In winter 1914, the practice was systematized and codified, if not industrialized with the use of modern materiel. Two trench networks were thus established, employing relatively similar methods, along a nearly continuous line from one end of the front to the other. From that point until the German offensive of spring 1918, this line of trenches would never shift more than thirty kilometres in any direction.

What explains the extraordinary effectiveness of such a system at this specific moment in the war?

Trench organization primarily varied by nationality. Despite the skill of their engineers, French trenches were rather perfunctory, especially at the start of the conflict. The general staff only reluctantly accepted the idea of trenches and did not wish its troops to get comfortable there. For Joffre, they were of only temporary utility, helping to minimize casualties (at least before the attack) while preparations were made for the assault that would allow a decisive breakthrough in the German lines.

On the German side, by contrast, the objective of entrenchment was to allow the troops to wait in the best possible conditions for Russia to collapse in the east. This outcome, in their view, would likely be followed by a negotiated peace in the west, as the Germans had already taken the northern coalfields and the iron and steel works of Lorraine in the first phase of the conflict. The aim was thus to hold the Western Front with a minimum of troops in order to free up the human resources needed to counter the massive Russian army on the Eastern Front. The German trenches were thus constructed with much care. They were deeply dug, with shelters on several levels. Wherever possible, they were gradually reinforced with concrete and sometimes also furnished with electricity and ventilation. These efforts were to be rewarded on the Somme in the summer of 1916.

Less perfunctory than that of the French but falling far short of the care shown by the Germans, British trench design reflected the high command's pragmatism. Conscious of the casualties entailed by all-out offensive, the British general staff was eager to conserve the strength of its expeditionary force, particularly as the losses inflicted on these experienced professional soldiers over the course of the war's first months had yet to be compensated for by the arrival of the volunteers of 1914 ('Kitchener's Army' or the 'New Army'), most of whom were still in training. Many British generals were ultimately in favour of waiting until the Royal Navy's (effective) blockade brought Germany to its knees or the Americans finally entered the conflict – which had been a conceivable scenario since the torpedoing of the *Lusitania* in May 1915, if not earlier.

Yet the basic organization of the trench system was the same on both sides of the front line: two lines of trenches separated by no man's land. Several hundred metres wide in flat, open country, sometimes just a few dozen in forested or steep terrain, it was covered by barbed-wire networks and contained several observation points for lookouts posted in advance of the front line. Never dug in a rectilinear manner, the trenches were crenellated so as to limit the danger of shrapnel and prevent enfilading fire should the enemy succeed in setting foot in them. They were generally organized according to the following model: a first-line trench, which the British called the 'fire trench'; a second-line trench some 200 metres behind; and what was known as a 'reserve' trench around 300 metres further back. All were linked by perpendicular communication saps. This in-depth organization allowed men and resources to be transported where they were needed, first-line troops to be regularly rotated to (relatively) unexposed positions and, in case the first line was taken by the enemy, an immediate counter-offensive to be launched from the second.

Cutting across it, the side of the trench facing the enemy included a fire step that allowed soldiers to fire from behind the protection of a sandbag parapet. The inner walls were reinforced with wooden boards, bundles of sticks or metal latticework. They were sufficiently deep to allow movement without the soldiers' heads being exposed. To make up for this protective depth, it was necessary to construct fire steps all along the trench. On the ground, duckboards more or less allowed the soldiers to move about without getting their feet wet. The chalky soil of the Somme and Champagne was the best suited from this point of view. The frequently soaked clay soil of the Nord-Pas-de-Calais area required the trenches' occupants to make their way through the mud for months on end. In cold and rainy periods, this resulted in a specific pathology, 'trench foot', which often developed into gangrene.

More generally, hygienic conditions were wanting nearly everywhere. Often, they were appalling. Crammed together and cooped up in the same clothes for long periods of time, the men were infested with lice. Rats thrived with the to and fro of supplies. In periods of intense fighting, the trenches were packed with cadavers and scattered pieces of flesh, which could not always be removed immediately. The continual, more or less frequent rotation of units was thus essential to ensuring that the men were able to continue fulfilling their duties as soldiers. They were rotated between the front line and the rear (generally located a few kilometres away in the first hamlet thought to be beyond artillery range) as well as between the first line and the support and reserve trenches of a given sector.

## THE OPERATION OF TRENCH SYSTEMS

While living conditions in the trenches were appalling, they had an essential advantage for the infantrymen: it was much harder to kill them there than in open terrain. They generally protected well against the direct fire of rifles and machine guns. As long as they were sufficiently deep and narrow, they were relatively effective against the shrapnel-type shells that exploded above the ground,[15] scattering large quantities of steel shot. By contrast, they only offered real protection against high-explosive shells[16] when equipped with concrete-reinforced shelters.

The first months of the war were its bloodiest: casualty rates actually began to decline in early 1915 and only once again rose when the war of movement resumed in spring 1918. In the interval, neither side ever decisively broke through the enemy's trench network. Each time that the exhausted and decimated attackers succeeded in taking a first line, they were subjected to immediate counter-attack by fresh troops from the second-line and reserve trenches. What's more, the attackers' artillery generally did a very poor job of accompanying the infantrymen's progress on the ground. Already complicated in static periods, it became nearly impossible to remain in liaison with the artillery once troops were on the move: telephone lines were difficult to lay during an assault and were frequently cut. Signalling with flags or lamps unduly exposed the signallers. Firing flares offered little information to observers and it was difficult to distinguish them from those that might have been fired by the other side. In fact, runners were most often used to deliver messages, a practice that entailed considerable uncertainty due to the need to return across the battlefield under enemy fire. This structural difficulty only began to be resolved with the appearance of motorized artillery – that is, tanks. Using tracks to move over terrain ravaged by bombardment and covered in armour to protect its operators, the tank allowed infantrymen to remain in contact with artillery.

The British and French first began to experiment with tank design independently of one another in 1915.[17] The earliest examples of tanks made their appearance on the Somme front in September 1916. But their initial use was disappointing: at once too heavy, too fragile, under-powered and insufficiently armed, these vehicles were prevented by design and production problems from achieving what was expected of them. It was only in the summer of 1918, with the introduction of the Renault light tank, that armoured vehicles began to be successfully used in large numbers by the Allies. On the German side, the use of tanks only truly reached maturity in June 1940, when they were deployed in close collaboration with the air force. By then, the French general staff had unfortunately converted to a defensive tactic relying on the ultimate line of trenches: the Maginot Line.

# CHAPTER 4

## THE TACTICAL CONTEXT: THE EVOLUTION OF ARMS BETWEEN 1914 AND 1916

On the Western Front, the transformation of a war of movement into a siege war spanning several hundred kilometres was to have a profound influence on the choice, design and use of weapons by the belligerents. Some of these weapons, including poison gas and flamethrowers, were relatively new. Others were significantly adapted versions of weapons that had been in use since the beginning of the modern era (grenades and mortars). Yet others seemed to have come straight out of the Middle Ages or even the Bronze Age (metal helmets, trench knives and so on). The arms in use at the start of hostilities (artillery and repeating rifles) were profoundly modified over the course of the conflict in terms of their use, capacity and design. Some of these developments were spurred on by general staffs, industrialists and scientists. Others, by contrast – mortars, grenade-launchers, knives for use in hand-to-hand combat, and so on – were introduced by 'do-it-yourselfers' in the trenches. Finally, several modern technologies – notably aviation, but also radio communication – underwent rapid development and transformation between August 1914 and November 1918.

From this point of view, the Battle of the Somme took place at a time when weapons systems and their use had already significantly evolved from the start of the war but had yet to reach the peak efficiency they were to attain in the summer of 1918. The still very inchoate development of communication and artillery-guidance technology particularly hampered the British offensive.

## New weapons

### Poison gas

In the late nineteenth century, the possibility that industrial gas (a fast-growing sector at the time) would be used for military purposes began to receive attention. Moreover, the 1899 Hague Convention specifically banned 'the use of projectiles the sole object of which is the diffusion of asphyxiating or deleterious gases'. Yet the Germans were unable to resist the temptation to deploy a weapon that allowed them to take advantage of their supremacy in the area of industrial chemistry.

On 22 April 1915, German sappers outside Ypres opened gas bottles in front of their lines. Designed for military use by one of Germany's most renowned chemists, Fritz Haber, the bottles were filled with a chlorine-based gas.[18] The wind pushed the heavy, yellow-green clouds towards the French lines. The effect was immediate: the French 'Turcos' (Algerian and Tunisian soldiers) fled their positions in disorder, as much out of surprise as because of the gas itself. With help from the soldiers of the 1st Australian Division, however, which was also attacked with gas on the 24th, the troops succeeded in stabilizing the front. Since the wind's orientation (direction and speed) did not always coincide with the attackers' objectives, later uses of poison gas were to prove even less conclusive. The mechanism for delivering the gas rapidly evolved towards the use of capsule-laden shells. On both sides, a complex dialectic developed between the various protective measures that were adopted (handkerchiefs and cotton wadding at first, then masks) and the trend towards ever more dangerous gases. Chlorine-based gases were rapidly replaced by chlorine-based gases supplemented with phosgene, which was yet more virulent than chlorine on its own. Finally, in 1917, what the Allies would call 'Yperite' or 'mustard gas' appeared. Its principal contribution was to strongly irritate all exposed skin while simultaneously affecting the lungs and eyes. As the regimental journal of a Scottish regiment, the Liverpool Scottish, noted with very British reserve: 'In these circumstances, the kilt is not an ideal garment.'[19]

That said, the use of gas never played a decisive role on the battlefield. It was tricky to use and could pose a risk to the attackers if the wind changed direction. Above all, the protective devices that were gradually implemented (from the first cotton wadding soaked in water and even urine to sophisticated gas masks) proved relatively effective, even if life under a gas mask was particularly uncomfortable. This discomfort was, moreover, shared between attackers and defenders, for the soldiers of a unit that used gas to facilitate its advance had to be equipped so as to endure its presence on the terrain to be occupied.

Over the course of the war, the psychological impact (on combatants as well as civilians) of poison gas was on the whole infinitely greater than its actual military impact. The conflict's iconography is particularly rich in images of soldiers, civilians (women and children) and even animals (such as horses) rigged out in strange, dehumanizing masks. One is struck by the representations of blinded soldiers as they make their way in long lines to the rear, each holding the shoulder of the man preceding him. And yet, in military terms, poison gas had only a limited impact over the course of the conflict, a fact that rendered its use all the crueller.

## Flamethrowers

While conflicts from antiquity to the Middle Ages[20] have witnessed the projection of burning liquids, the German army was the first to develop a genuine 'flamethrower' (*Flammenwerfer*) in the years immediately preceding the war. The Germans first used it before the French positions at Maricourt – that is, on the Somme – in March 1915.

As with poison gas, the use of flamethrowers was to have a major psychological impact but be of relatively little military value. For operating them was a difficult and dangerous task for the attackers. These weapons are used at close range and the individual who carries the heavy and bulky unit is particularly exposed to enemy fire, with potentially lethal consequences for himself and those near him. Finally, in the event of capture, the flamethrower's operator was rarely spared by the enemy...

### THE EVOLUTION OF MACHINE GUNS AND ARTILLERY

Machine guns and artillery were present in large numbers from the start of the conflict. Over its course, however, their use and design were transformed in opposite directions: while machine guns became easier to operate and move forward in support of an attack, the artillery migrated to ever more remote positions on the battlefield, employed ever larger calibres and increasingly relied on curved rather than direct fire in response to what had become a situation of siege warfare.

From the start of the conflict, Hotchkiss, Maxim and Saint-Étienne machine guns were part of the belligerents' arsenal and immediately showed themselves to be remarkably effective. The basic model used by the British army was manufactured by Vickers and featured a water-cooling system.[21] When there were enough of them to cover the length of a battlefield, their rate of fire (400–600 shots per minute) effectively prevented enemy troops from advancing without cover, especially if effectual firing positions had been established in advance. The carnage visited upon the British assault waves on 1 July 1916 was mainly the work of efficient German machine-gun fire. Throughout the conflict, improvements were made to increase the efficiency of these weapons systems. This was primarily a matter of improving reliability: preventing mechanical failures in the cycling of ammunition, introducing suitable cooling mechanisms (air or water) to prevent barrels from overheating and reducing the weight of the device. Their operators had to handle and sometimes move what were at first very heavy machines. To ensure that the gun could maintain a nearly continuous rate of fire, replacement parts (barrels in particular) and huge quantities of ammunition needed to be kept available nearby, further weighing down its operators. On the battlefield, what's more, the group made up by the machine gun and its operators, together with their equipment and ammunition, was a priority target for the enemy's direct and indirect fire. It was thus necessary to reserve firing positions for machine guns that were relatively well protected by the landscape or suitable fortifications (such as bunkers). Having already spent many months in the same spot, the German defenders of the Somme were from this point of view able to select and prepare ideal positions in relative peace.

In 1914, the French army had set off to war with equipment of which it was proud: the centrepiece of its artillery stock, the 75-mm gun, was a modern weapon that was capable (over a short period) of firing between 15 and 20 shells per minute at a distance of more than eight kilometres. Its hydraulic break allowed it to engage in continuous fire without requiring the gun to be retrained with each shot. Like its German 77-mm counterpart, its direct, rapid and accurate fire on targets in view of its gunners made it the ideal weapon for closely accompanying attackers in a war of movement. Since 1904, the main British field gun had been the '18-pounder gun'. Slightly larger in calibre (84 mm) than the French and German guns, it fired a heavier shell but at a somewhat less rapid rate.

Once operations had become bogged down in trench warfare, the use of artillery utterly changed. Field artillery now had to move back and from a more distant position seek to strike far-removed enemy defences with indirect fire. Henceforth, enemy targets were rarely in direct view; often, they were located on the opposite slope. Successfully zeroing in on targets thus became an increasingly painstaking exercise and their identification required a combination of terrestrial and aerial means (observers, balloons, dirigibles and, with time, aeroplanes). Successful bombardment thus came to depend on the level of training received by gunners and observers. At the same time, heavier calibre guns were increasingly used to send ever larger explosive charges ever greater distances. These guns were complex machines and took a long time to manufacture. From the conflict's outset, naval and fortress guns – those of forts Vaux and Douaumont, for example – were transferred to the front. The evolution of artillery – from light field canon to heavy long-range guns – reached its peak with the development of guns mounted on railway wagons. Between May and August 1918, the four German howitzers mistakenly known as 'Big Berthas' that had been installed in the Aisne regularly bombarded Paris with 125-kilogram shells at a range of 140 kilometres.[22]

In contrast to field artillery, an entire segment of trench artillery was miniaturized and brought closer to the line of fire. This was the case of the curved-fire howitzers with which German troops were abundantly supplied from the start of the conflict. It was also the case of mortars – the small, ultralight guns meant to be used by one trench against another. These weapons (the German *Minenwerfer*, French *crapouillots* and British Stokes mortar) were developed as much by do-it-yourself engineers in the trenches as by national arsenals. Finally, there was the reappearance of the hand grenade, the ultimate development in the miniaturization of artillery. A grenade is essentially a small quantity of explosives thrown towards the enemy by either rifle shot or, more often, the simple strength of the soldier's arm. Its widespread and growing use by the infantry (France's *grenadiers-voltigeurs*) came to symbolize the types of combat that the conflict had engendered.

Between 1914 and 1916, however, the artillery's real problem was not simply a matter of qualitative transformation, of light and mobile direct-fire guns yielding to heavy indirect-fire ones. The main problem was quantitative: how to rapidly and massively increase the production of shells. No one had foreseen that the conflict would last so long or that the rate of fire would become so high for such long periods. In both France and Great Britain, it was necessary to take emergency measures in the autumn of 1914 to address the inadequate stockpiles of shells: specialized munitions factory workers were called back, female employees were recruited and production lines were set up in workshops not intended for that purpose. Under the impetus of energetic political leaders (Lloyd George in Great Britain, Albert Thomas in France), these shortfalls were gradually reduced, beginning in late 1915 in France and a year later in Britain. The tremendous effort expended to increase the total production of ammunition came at the cost of quality, particularly in the British case. As an industrial process, the manufacture of artillery shells is more complicated than it appears, especially in what concerns the precise operation of the detonator.

# CHAPTER 5

## THE CREATION OF A BRITISH 'NEW ARMY'

The scale of British casualties on 1 July 1916 was primarily due to the unprecedented number of troops sent into battle on that day.

Great Britain had a long military tradition. It was on the strength of this that, with assistance from the Royal Navy, it had carved out an immense empire spanning every continent. But it had always relied on a ground army of limited size, exclusively made up of professional soldiers. Protected by its island status and navy, Britain had not been invaded since 1066. Unlike France, it had never had to rely on mass conscription or, later, the draft to build an army capable of defending thousands of kilometres of land frontiers against one or more Continental adversaries. The only armies that had clashed on British soil did so in the context of internecine English (the Wars of the Roses, the English Civil War) and intra-British wars (the English vs the Irish or the English vs the Scots). The troops who fought in North America, Spain, India, Sudan, Afghanistan, South Africa, and so on were all men who had enlisted, often for long periods, in a small but mobile professional army that could be rapidly transported by ship throughout the entire world.

Once Napoleon had been defeated, the British Army of the nineteenth century focused its activity (with the exception of the Crimean War) on a series of colonial expeditions in Asia and Africa. On each occasion, its mobility, professionalism and, above all, firepower rapidly gave it a decisive advantage. The striking exception was the Boer War (1899–1902), during which the British faced off against Transvaal and the Orange Free State. For once, it found itself confronted by a similarly mobile army of European origin that, mainly thanks to Kaiser Wilhelm II of Germany, was equipped with modern weapons. The conflict's early setbacks – pitched battles followed by a well-organized guerrilla campaign – forced the British army to modify somewhat its organization and mode of operation. If one counts the contributions of contingents from the Dominions of Australia, New Zealand and Canada – yet another innovation – it was the first time since the Napoleonic Wars that British forces had exceeded 400,000 men. Most of Britain's First World War military leaders, Kitchener and Haig foremost among them, had thus fought in southern Africa fifteen years earlier. Following the conflict, the Conservative government launched a series of reforms intended to improve the soldiers' equipment, the officers' professionalism and the operation of territorial units. At a time when the development of the German Imperial Navy required that investment be focused on the Royal Navy, however, budgetary constraints limited the scale and implementation of these reforms.

It was this professional army that, in August 1914, provided the six divisions and 120,000 men of the British Expeditionary

Force in France. Very rapidly transferred to France and Belgium, these soldiers fought with formidable efficiency from the earliest days of the 'Battle of the Frontiers', which began on 20 August 1914. Thanks to its rapid, accurate and effective marksmanship, the BEF inflicted very high casualties on the German infantry at Mons, during the withdrawal from Le Cateau and outside the Belgian enclave of Ypres. Always outnumbered, British troops had carried the day in all of their nineteenth-century colonial wars with their powerful and accurate shooting skills. In France, by contrast, a deeply rooted intellectual dogma (that of the 'all-out offensive', or *offensive à outrance*) and particularly tight budgetary constraints had combined to favour training recruits to throw themselves, bayonets fixed, on straw dummies instead of advancing in formation while firing their rapid and accurate (but costly in ammunition) Lebel rifles.

In early 1914, the size of the British army (400,000 men total, including territorial reserve units consisting of soldiers who had left active service) prevented it from assembling the number of soldiers necessary to operate at parity with the French army, which following mobilization numbered nearly 3 million men. Nor were all of its troops available for deployment to the Continent: some regular troops had to remain at crucial colonial posts (such as India) and a portion of the territorial units stayed behind to defend the national territory against a (hypothetical) German invasion.[23] At its origins, the BEF thus consisted of a small army of experienced professional soldiers. From a geographical point of view, its natural area of deployment was near the Channel ports, at the western edge of the French operation. After the 'Race to the Sea' and the excavation of trench networks in autumn 1914 had durably stabilized the front along an unbroken line running from the North Sea to the Vosges, British troops, with support from Belgian soldiers and French Navy Riflemen, set about defending the unoccupied strip of Belgian territory around the fortified camp of Ypres as well as a portion of the Nord-Pas-de-Calais area.


The remarkable influx of more than 1 million volunteers in 1914 (out of nearly 2.5 million between 1914 and 1916) should have allowed the British general staff to dispatch vast human resources to the Western Front. Yet it would be long before anything of the kind happened. In addition to the regular army, the general mobilization in France had immediately called up twenty age cohorts. These troops had already been trained in the use of arms by two years of mandatory military service as well as frequent periods in reserve. They knew how to use the weapons given them and how to manoeuvre in coordinated units, and were still imbued with military codes and discipline. At mobilization, what's more, their weapons, uniforms and supplies were waiting ready for them, having generally (if not always) been stockpiled in the appropriate quantities. Nothing like that existed on the British side in August 1914.

The men who volunteered in summer 1914 did so for the duration of the war and at a time when almost no one imagined that it might last more than four years. This is one reason for the throngs that showed up at recruitment centres in August. The minister of war, Lord Kitchener, was a notable exception. From the start of hostilities, he was convinced that the war might last a long time. This is why he pushed for the creation of a mass army. In what came to be the best-known (and most copied) recruitment poster of all time, Kitchener's severe, moustachioed face is pictured above outstretched arm, his finger pointing at the potential recruit. The vast majority of those who enlisted thought that the hostilities would be over by Christmas and wanted to have a chance to participate in them.

Over the course of August and September, these men would become aware of the inadequate space in the barracks and the fact that uniforms, various types of equipment and individual weapons were lacking. There were not enough experienced soldiers to supervise and train all of the recruits, some of whom were very young or very old. Together, they represented a cross section of British society: city-dwellers and country people, workers and employees, members of the lumpenproletariat and students from the country's elite public schools. With the exception of a small number who had graduated from public schools offering officer-cadet training, what they all had in common (apart from their enthusiasm and immense willingness) was a near-total lack of military training. The instructors who should have trained them were for the most part already with the BEF fighting in France – where they had suffered significant casualties, what's more. Once the French front had stabilized in autumn 1914, a number of experienced NCOs and other personnel were brought back to Great Britain, where they began shaping the 'pals battalions', consisting of men who had jointly enlisted along geographical or professional lines. This came to be known as 'the New Army' or 'Kitchener's Army', in reference to its architect. But training hundreds of thousands of men took a great deal of time, especially given that, after more than a century of industrial revolution in England, the young men of the working classes were in poor physical condition: the mean height of recruits in 1914 – 1.67 metres – is testimony to this.[24] In the war's first weeks, nearly a third of volunteers were rejected after medical examination. At the strategic level, finally, it gradually became clear that the British general staff, which had become accustomed to manoeuvring small mobile units over the course of colonial expeditions, lacked the experience needed to oversee successfully a mass army in a European theatre.

When would this 'New Army' be ready to intervene on the Western Front? Not in 1915, at any rate, for in the course of that year the British government had adopted the bold idea of its young First Lord of the Admiralty, Winston Churchill. Rather than joining the French army in Joffre's extraordinarily bloody attempts to break through the German front in northern and eastern France by sending division after division into battle, why not attempt to win the war by relying on a major strategic advantage: the Royal Navy?

By taking the straits of the Dardanelles separating the Mediterranean from the Black Sea and threatening Constantinople, British troops would be able to force Turkey to abandon its alliance with Germany, encourage the Balkan countries to join the Allies and link up with the Russian army. In addition to the large French contingent that was to serve as an occupation force,[25] the plan relied upon the troops of the 'Kitchener Battalions' as well as volunteers from the far-off Dominions of Australia and New Zealand, who were then en route to the battlefields. Should the plan succeed, Germany and Austria would find themselves encircled and have no choice but to relinquish the fight.

This ambitious scheme was not to succeed. Like all First World War operations that sought to circumvent the enemy, the attempted breakthrough in the Dardanelles and subsequent landing at Gallipoli ended in failure. By December 1915, the last Allied troops had left the Suvla Bay peninsula. The last units, among them the Newfoundland Regiment, re-embarked from Cape Helles on the night of 8–9 January 1916. Following this setback, Churchill resigned and began one of his many periods in the political wilderness, though he briefly participated as an infantry regiment colonel in the Battle of the Somme.

In the meantime, the French army was nearly alone in shouldering the burden of the major offensives conducted on the Western Front to win victory for the Allies by breaking through the German lines. In 1915, two major offensives took place, in Artois and Champagne. Conceived and carried out under the authority of Joffre, who had won glory at the Battle of the Marne, the offensives were very costly failures. As always in this conflict, direct assaults by grouped infantry against entrenched fortifications defended by units possessing modern firepower ended in bloody failure for the attackers. This reality first emerged in August 1914 with the Battle of the Frontiers – the bloodiest of the entire war. It was 1915, however, that was to be the war's bloodiest year due to the frequency and intensity of French infantry assaults.[26] If total mortality for Great Britain (astronomical though it was) was significantly lower than that for France, it is because fewer British and Dominion troops participated in the battles of the Western Front in 1915 than would be the case later in the war. Taken together, the two armies mobilized around 8.5 million men. Yet while the British lost around 870,000 men between 1914 and 1918, deaths on the French side were around 1.4 million.

# CHAPTER 6

## PREPARING THE BRITISH BATTLE PLAN FOR 1 JULY 1916

Responsibility for preparing the July 1916 British offensive mainly fell to two men: Sir Douglas Haig, who had succeeded General French as chief of the general staff in December 1915, and Sir Henry Rawlinson, commander of the Fourth Army.

The two men knew one another well and had worked together (as army commander and chief of staff, respectively) during the main British battles in France in 1915: Neuve-Chapelle, Aubers Ridge and Loos. The lessons they drew from these engagements – and their failure – were to shape their doctrine in the Somme offensive. Yet neither gave sufficient attention to what were to prove critical issues on 1 July. Finally, their debate regarding the first day's objectives reflected major disagreement within the British general staff concerning the strategic objective of the entire offensive.

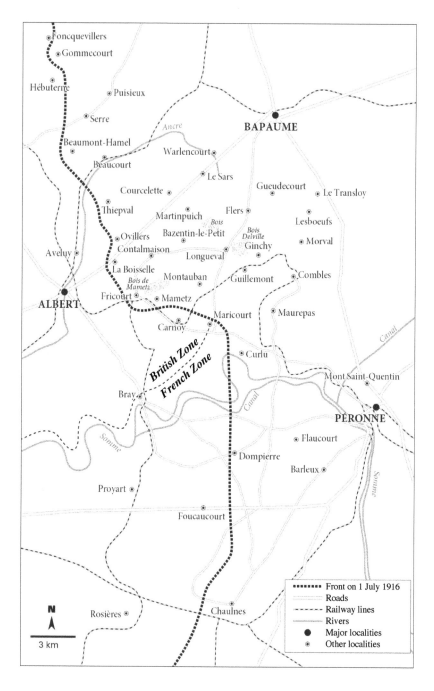

THE SOMME FRONT BETWEEN GOMMECOURT AND PÉRONNE
ON THE MORNING OF 1 JULY 1916

## ACKNOWLEDGING THE PRIMACY OF ARTILLERY ON THE BATTLEFIELD

On the basis of British army operations in 1915 and their observation of those of the French, which had cost so many human lives, Haig and Rawlinson were convinced of the now established primacy of artillery: 'Artillery conquers, infantry occupies.' The planned operation therefore relied on an intense artillery bombardment lasting several days that, by virtue of its duration and intensity, would annihilate the German infantry in its trenches. British troops would merely need to advance – at a walk – to occupy enemy terrain, thus emptied of soldiers capable of fighting.

For this reason, it was decided that it would be of little use to employ smokescreens, much less poison gas. Where possible, by contrast, saps[27] were dug under the German positions and mines placed there. The chalky soil of the Somme was well suited for cutting tunnels, and many new recruits, particularly among the Welsh, had been miners in civilian life.

Moreover, the 1915 offensives and particularly Neuve-Chapelle had convinced the British generals that it was necessary to advance over a broad front at least twenty kilometres long. Given the continuity of the lines, a successful breakthrough at any one spot exposed the attackers to the possibility of flanking fire from enemy units located on either side of the breakthrough zone. Attacking along a broad front, by contrast, allowed such flanking attacks to be kept out of range of the units spearheading the offensive.

As a consequence, it was decided that British troops would attack along a front of more than twenty-five kilometres, not counting the additional ten-kilometre front assigned the French troops on the British army's right. Their advance would follow several days of bombardment intended to destroy the German trenches and fortifications, silence their machine-gun nests and pulverize their barbed-wire networks. More than 1,100 field guns equivalent in calibre to the French 75-mm were earmarked for this purpose, as were 400 pieces of heavy artillery ranging in calibre from 90 to 420 mm (navy guns).

In what was yet another innovation, the artillery barrage was to adjust its range in keeping with a precise timetable determined by the troops' expected rate of advance. In this way, the infantry would be assured cover as it moved forward over enemy terrain. Since it was assumed that the preliminary bombardment would destroy the Germans' advance positions, the progress of artillery fire could be anticipated by reference to the infantry's theoretical walking tempo.

## NEGLECTED QUESTIONS: HOW TO SILENCE THE GERMAN BATTERIES AND ADVANCE OVER NO MAN'S LAND?

The formula cited above – 'artillery conquers, infantry occupies' – presupposes that the latter can advance without incident once the enemy's first lines have been destroyed. But what happens when the German army possesses powerful long-range artillery behind the first two lines, as was the case on the Somme in mid-1916 – artillery precisely intended to check the advance of enemy foot soldiers and support possible counter-attacks?

While it is true that the power of German artillery on the Somme was not entirely disregarded by the British general staff, they clearly underestimated it. Only guns considered unnecessary to crushing the trenches – or around 180 relatively old artillery pieces out of a total of roughly 1500 – were allocated to counter-battery fire against the German artillery.

The question also arose as to how to reconnoitre and identify long-range German artillery located several kilometres behind the lines. For it to be accurate, this type of long-distance fire requires particularly precise targeting procedures relying on aerial observation. Two conditions, in turn, must be met if such observation is to be effective: control of the sky and good weather.

Finally, how was British infantry to cross the distance separating the opposing trenches? At a walk? By running? By leaps and bounds? In a line? By skirmishing groups? Haig and Rawlinson believed that the troops they were sending into battle that day, most of whom had volunteered in 1914 and lacked prior military experience, were likely to become dangerously disorganized if asked to advance other than by forming lines and walking forward... and a disorganized troop can no longer be effectively commanded by its officers. This choice considerably increased the time needed to cross the battlefield and forced the soldiers to adopt an upright posture that would maximally expose them to German fire in the event that, despite the initial artillery preparation, the latter were still capable of riposting to the attack when the time came.

## The ambiguities of the British plan in regards to the offensive's objectives

Throughout preparations for the offensive, a debate took shape between Haig, who was trained as a cavalry officer, and Rawlinson, an infantry officer. What should the British forces' objective be for the first day of the attack? Rawlinson pushed for the near-total conquest of the enemy's first line, or an average advance of around 1,100 metres. Haig, for his part, was firmly in favour of aiming, not just for the first line of German trenches, but also for the second, or an average advance of around 2,200 metres. In operational terms, the difference was far from trivial: an effort to reach the second position required that all objectives be eliminated in two lines of trenches, not just one. With the same number of guns and shells, it was thus necessary to destroy roughly twice as many targets, which would automatically entail a 50 per cent reduction in the density of fire directed against the enemy. What's more, adding further objectives located at a greater remove reduced the likelihood of accurate fire, another factor that accounts for the diminished effectiveness of the preliminary bombardment.

In fact, the debate regarding the British forces' objective for the first day of the offensive reflected deep disagreement over the real goal of the operation. In seeking to break through the German lines deeply, Haig hoped to clear a space through which the cavalry could successfully rush. On the map, he had located a favourable sector north of Pozières. If the British cavalry broke through here, it might be possible to take Bapaume (twenty kilometres away) rapidly, and from there threaten Arras. Taking the town would create a salient, forcing the Germans to withdraw large numbers of troops in the north and south to straighten the front line. It would force them, in short, to begin a retreat...

Rawlinson, for his part, was convinced that, given the effectiveness of the German defences, it was necessary to advance by way of a series of moderate and successive gains (a tactic he described as 'bite and hold'). Every time a position was won, it would have to be reinforced against inevitable German counter-attack. In his view, any operation that sought to create a strategic breakthrough of enemy lines was illusory and dangerous: at this stage of the conflict, the difficulties involved in rapidly dispatching – over long distances and under fire – the reinforcements, ammunition and rations necessary for such a rapid breakthrough were simply too great. Rawlinson's objective was gradually to exhaust the German army, forcing it to relax its pressure on Verdun by obliging it to transfer troops and guns to the Somme.

Between January and June, the debate raged within

the British general staff while evolving in tandem with developments at Verdun. As so often, it ended in a relatively opaque compromise: the operational objectives would be more or less those favoured by Rawlinson, though they would remain to some degree subject to the discretion of Haig, his hierarchical superior. At the same time, a great deal of tactical leeway would be left to subordinates in the field. Haig, for his part, was to hold two divisions of cavalry in reserve on 1 July. Astride their mounts, sabres drawn, they waited from dawn and for the rest of the morning for the order to rush forward.

Finally, the question arose as to the hour at which the troops were to set off: should they attack at dawn, around 4.30, or instead at 7.30 (and thus in the full daylight of a July morning)? In order to make it easier for senior officers to observe the troops' progress and increase the accuracy of artillery fire, the decision was made to opt for the later hour. The British soldiers were thus to manoeuvre in full view of their adversaries should the latter have nevertheless made it to their firing positions.

# CHAPTER 7

## THE FRENCH BATTLE PLAN ON THE SOMME

1915 was a catastrophic year for the French army. Despite great loss of life and Joffre's many bloody offensives, nothing had succeeded in driving the Germans back from their positions in France, much less in breaking through the front. Over the course of the first seventeen months of the war, nearly 2 million French soldiers had been killed, wounded or taken prisoner.

### THE CONDUCT OF THE WAR BY FRENCH LEADERS IN EARLY 1916

At year's end, politicians for the first time began to wonder about casualty levels and to criticize more or less openly the conduct of operations under Joffre. Until then, the latter had benefited in public opinion and among politicians from his status as the 'Victor of the Marne'. In the summer of 1915, the president of the Republic, Henri Poincaré, asked the minister of war, Alexandre Millerand, to supply him with an inventory of losses. This had never been done before and, in his memoirs, Poincaré speaks of his feelings of anxious consternation faced with the figures that it revealed.[28] The politicians, soldiers and civilians of 1914 expected that any European conflict conducted with modern weapons would be bloody. Partly for this reason, however, everyone believed that it would be of short duration.

Prime minister since November 1915, Aristide Briand had lost confidence in Joffre but did not dare run the political risk of replacing him. This was doubly the case for the new minister of war, Joseph Gallieni (Joffre's superior during the Madagascar campaign). Joffre was popular: on the basis of the 'taxis of the Marne' episode, public opinion credited him with an important role in the battle as commander of the entrenched camp of Paris.[29] But Gallieni was sick, weakened by the bladder cancer that was to kill him in May 1916. Under the Third Republic's division of powers, what's more, decisions as to the conduct of wartime operations were to be taken by the chief of staff – that is, Joffre.

The decision reached by the French and British soldiers and politicians who met at Chantilly in December 1915 to launch a major joint offensive thus reflected a collective desire to rapidly (and victoriously) put an end to a conflict that, by dragging on, had begun to exhaust national economies and populations. Many in the British government, however – first and foremost Kitchener – would have preferred to wait longer before sending so many inexperienced troops into battle. But there was significant French pressure for British troops to do their part on the Western Front. Whether out of a sense of fair play or genuine conviction, Haig proved receptive to the arguments of Joffre, with whom he got along well.

## THE CONSEQUENCES OF THE GERMAN OFFENSIVE ON VERDUN

The German offensive of February 1916 further weakened Joffre's position. This attack had not been sufficiently anticipated. Defences had not been well prepared and the first days of the battle revealed serious tactical errors, resulting among other things in the fall of Fort Douaumont. Newly promoted generals such as Robert Nivelle (in charge of artillery) and Philippe Pétain (given command of the Verdun front) won fame for themselves. If Joffre survived in his position through the spring, it was above all for fear that replacing him mid-battle would have been taken as a demoralizing sign by the public and jeopardized Briand's majority in the Chamber of Deputies.

In this context, the idea of conducting an offensive on the Somme was once again endorsed in March. Several times, however, the pressure on Verdun led the French commander to urge his British ally to push forward the date for the offensive, to which end he adduced two arguments:

- It was becoming increasingly urgent to launch an offensive on the Somme, if only to encourage the Germans to withdraw troops and material from Verdun.
- As time passed, ever fewer French troops would be available to participate in a joint offensive. While the rapid rotation of units had led the German general staff to overestimate French casualties, they were nevertheless very high and the rotation system, or *tourniquet*, required a vast number of troops to be held in reserve between their short (but frequent) stints at the front line.

The same debate roiled the French and British general staffs: should the planned offensive seek to break through the German front and thereby win the war? Or should it rather seek to wear down the enemy and force him to transfer resources from Verdun?

In charge of Verdun as chief of Army Group Centre, Pétain did not understand why the French army would divert some of its own human and material resources to a new front. Why not let the British with their fresh troops go it alone? And as soon as possible! But such an attitude made Joffre bristle: what if, against all expectations, the British broke through the German front? All of the glory of victory would be theirs, an unthinkable outcome! The commander of Army Group North and thus of the future Somme front (Ferdinand Foch), as well as that of the Sixth Army (Émile Fayolle), which was to carry out the attack, were for their part increasingly beset by doubts. At the start of the year, Foch had counted on attacking along a forty-kilometre front with more than 40 divisions and 1,700 pieces of artillery. As 1 July approached and the number of troops available to him diminished, he began to lose confidence in what could be accomplished by the operation.

### THE FRENCH PLAN OF ATTACK ON THE SOMME

Yet, despite the concentration of French efforts on Verdun, the human and material resources allocated for the Somme offensive were far from insignificant in either quantitative or qualitative terms. In what concerned troop numbers, Joffre and Foch (commander of Army Group North)[30] ultimately committed three army corps (or eight divisions)[31] – the 20th, 25th and the Colonial Corps – to the joint offensive. They were merged into the Sixth Army, command of which was given to General Fayolle, an artilleryman. An additional army corps, the 2nd, was to be held nearby in reserve. These were all experienced troops. In September 1914, the 20th Corps under Foch's command had stopped the German army's invasion outside Nancy and was rightly considered an elite group. Though it was not to take part in the battle on 1 July, the Tenth Army (led by General Joseph Alfred Micheler), with its five army corps, would be stationed a little further to the rear.

The French troops were distributed between the northern and southern banks of the Somme. In the north, the 20th Corps held the extreme right in the plan of attack, adjoining the British troops near Maricourt. In the south, the two other army corps were ranged to Foucaucourt-en-Santerre.

Relative to its numbers and the width of its front, the Sixth Army was well supplied with artillery (more than 1,000 pieces), particularly heavy artillery (around 600 pieces). Given the narrowness of its front of attack, the density of French artillery was superior to that of the British. The French gunners were also more experienced than their British counterparts. French aviation also dominated its German adversary in numerical terms and with regards to the performance of its aircraft. Furthermore, the German fortifications facing the French troops had been less carefully reinforced over the course of the preceding months, a reflection of the German command's scepticism regarding France's capacity to conduct an offensive elsewhere than Verdun. For this reason, German efforts to consolidate their lines in spring 1916 were much less intense in the French sector than in the British. Despite alarming reports from German intelligence regarding French preparations, the high command remained incredulous to the last: in contrast to the British, the French benefited from a quite improbable element of surprise on 1 July. With experienced troops and significant heavy artillery, they thus attacked an enemy that was not really expecting them.

# CHAPTER 8

## THE GERMAN ARMY ON THE SOMME IN 1916

### THE EVOLUTION OF GERMAN STRATEGY

Following the failure of Helmuth von Moltke's offensive on the Marne, which sought to rapidly break the French army before the Russian army achieved full strength, the front stabilized in October 1914. Once Moltke had been replaced as chief of staff by Falkenhayn, the German high command immediately adapted to the new situation and completely revised its strategy. Henceforth, the German army would adopt an essentially defensive posture on the Western Front, seeking to force the enemy – above all, at this stage, France – to sue for peace. If this was not to be had through victory in a decisive battle, it would be brought about by the attrition of France's troops, the exhaustion of its natural resources and the collapse of its people's morale. This feeling of confidence was reflected in German responses to the overtures of neutral countries as they sounded out the belligerents regarding acceptable terms for a negotiated peace.[32]

\* \* \*

Among German leaders, several considerations bolstered this choice of strategy:

First of all, even though the initial Russian offensive in East Prussia in August 1914 had been crushed at Tannenberg by the future Marshal Hindenburg, the Eastern Front remained active. Given the front's expanse, the size of the Russian army and the frequent shortcomings of its Austro-Hungarian ally, the German army was forced to devote significant human and material resources to it.

Next, in the course of its orderly and methodical withdrawal from the Marne, the German army selected the most favourable places for mounting an effective defence: ridge lines and sometimes opposite slopes when they offered a strategic advantage. This allowed it to halt its retreat and begin digging trenches and fortifications.

Finally, this practice was perfectly understood and accepted by German infantrymen. Contrary to what everyone had expected at the outset, the war continued beyond Christmas 1914, with fighting taking place deep within French territory rather than near the Rhine. German infantrymen were thus aware of the ravages that war visited on territories and populations and were relieved to know their loved ones had been spared such an ordeal.

## 1915

From a strategic point of view, 1915 was a successful year for Germany on both the Western and Eastern fronts. Despite massive and repeated French offensives in Artois and Champagne, the German line of defence was never truly breached. The more limited British attacks at Neuve-Chapelle and elsewhere were similarly driven back.

More resources had been devoted to the German trench and fortification systems and they were more complete and extensive as a result. They were generally constructed by the troops who had been assigned to occupy them (rather than by older territorial units, as in the French case). The deeper German shelters were thus often made of concrete and protected by dense barbed-wire networks. What's more, in constructing these physical defences, special attention was given to establishing well-protected and surplus lines of communication (buried telephone lines, in particular). Artillery batteries located behind defensive lines were installed with much care and the firing coordinates of no man's land and the enemy's first lines precisely noted. The German military doctrine of the time called for rapid counter-attack with all available resources in the event that the enemy succeeded in gaining a foothold in the trenches: it was thus the artillery's role to prevent the attackers from being supplied with fresh troops, supplies and ammunition. Under a deluge of shells, they were instead to face nearly immediate counter-attack.

As well as resulting in virtually no territorial gains, the French and British offensives of 1915 were catastrophic for the attackers in terms of casualties. As I have already noted, 1915 was to prove the conflict's deadliest year for the French army – deadlier than 1917, the year of the Chemin des Dames offensive, and deadlier even than 1916, that of the battles of Verdun and the Somme. Due to the smaller number of troops involved, British casualties were not as heavy in absolute terms. And yet those who fell were experienced professional soldiers of the BEF and the fighting ability of the British army was undermined by their loss. The experienced soldiers killed in 1915 would be further missed when the time came to train that year's new recruits and lead them into battle a year later. For it was only starting in mid-1915 that the troops of 'Kitchener's Army' began to arrive in France, and since they lacked previous military experience, many months would be necessary to supply the men who enlisted in the summer and autumn of 1914 with even basic training.

Though significant in absolute terms, German casualties were nevertheless around half those suffered by the French and British attackers, a reflection of the decisive advantage conferred by a defensive strategy at this stage in the conflict.

## German strategy for 1916

Despite the success of its strategy, the German general staff was also concerned about the level of casualties in what had become a stalemate on the Western Front. As the warring parties' economies began to adapt to the needs for equipment and ammunition, it seemed increasingly unlikely that the war would end anytime soon. In August 1914, everyone expected the war to be over by Christmas. By late 1915, the general staffs began to fear that it would continue for several years, with losses that would seem intolerable to even the most resilient civilian populations.

It was in response to such concerns that, at their December 1915 conference in Chantilly, the Allies decided to organize joint (French and British) and simultaneous (on the Italian and Eastern fronts) offensives for the purpose of achieving decisive victory. On the German side, Falkenhayn was also eager to force the hand of destiny. He was concerned about German military demography, which was inferior to that of the Entente powers. Even though he did not have a high opinion of the military skills of British 'New Army' soldiers, he feared the arrival of these additional troops. He also realized that the Allied general staffs were capable of gradually learning from their failures and would eventually launch better-prepared attacks along larger fronts in coordination with artillery. Hence his decision to (partly) break with his defensive tactic and launch a major offensive against Verdun.

It remains a matter of debate as to whether Falkenhayn truly hoped to break through the French front, cross the Meuse and achieve a decisive victory. If so, the subsequent portrayal of his objective as an effort to 'bleed the French army white' is no more than *ex post facto* window dressing for an operation that failed in its first phase. Either way, the German leaders expected the Battle of Verdun to lead a defeated and exhausted French army to ask politicians for a negotiated end to the fighting.[33]

With the fighting still under way in June, Falkenhayn had to contemplate the possibility of an Allied offensive on the Western Front to relieve Verdun. Yet he regarded the prospect of a joint Franco-British offensive as highly unlikely. Given the intensity of fighting at Verdun, he believed that the French army at this stage no longer possessed a reserve of men capable of being sent into battle on a new front. Observing French divisions freshly arrived at the front melt away after a few days, Falkenhayn concluded that they had been destroyed. While these troops did indeed suffer heavy casualties, what he in fact witnessed (but not really understood) were the workings of the French general staff's rotation system. At the price of immense logistical effort,[34] this ultra-rapid rotation of units allowed the troops to be relieved before their morale and physical condition had been totally exhausted.

Thus overestimating French casualties, Falkenhayn was convinced that only the British were capable of launching an offensive in 1916. He further believed that it would take place not on the Somme, but rather in the Pas-de-Calais, where their logistical bases and most experienced troops were located.

## THE GERMAN COMMAND ON THE SOMME

General Fritz von Below, commander of the German Second Army stationed on the Somme, noted that, beginning in mid-1915, British units had begun gradually to relieve the French units that had been stationed there since autumn 1914. In March 1915, he asked for a pre-emptive offensive to be launched against the army he saw gathering before him. His request, which would have had the consequence of diverting troops and materiel from the Verdun front, was initially ignored by Falkenhayn. Von Below thus embarked, *faute de mieux*, on an effort to consolidate massively his lines and fortifications. Shelters were reinforced, barbed-wire networks made denser. Nearly everywhere, a shift took place to a double belt of barbed wire, each section of which was around ten metres thick and separated from the next by fifteen metres. To this was added a third line of defences to be dug behind the first two.

Faced with growing signs that a British offensive was in the works, in early June Below reiterated his request for a pre-emptive attack. Bogged down at Verdun, Falkenhayn began to consider the matter, but the start of the Russian offensive on the Eastern Front (the 'Brusilov Offensive') required him to send emergency reinforcements there.[35] Von Below had to make do with four additional infantry divisions (or nearly 60,000 men nevertheless) as well as a number of new heavy artillery guns, which arrived just before the start of the British offensive.

It was the 20th German Reserve Corps that would endure the brunt of the British assault. Its leader, Lieutenant General Hermann von Stein, was a dynamic career soldier. After having given his full attention to preparing the defences of the entire Second Army, he took extraordinary measures to maintain his troops' offensive spirit. They were encouraged to patrol no man's land constantly and conduct surprise raids against enemy trenches at all hours of the day and night. Gathered together in an ad hoc manual, his methods were soon adopted as a model for the entire German army. In particular, they allowed him to gather precise information as to the imminence of the British attack.

His efforts paid off: on 1 July 1916, British troops were to confront well-trained German soldiers in good morale sheltering behind dense and effective defences.

# CHAPTER 9

## PREPARATIONS FOR THE 1 JULY 1916 ATTACK

Beginning in the autumn of 1915, British troops, most of them veterans of the BEF, began to relieve the French units holding the Somme front. Facing them were the German troops stationed there since the winter of 1914.

### THE MONTHS PRECEDING THE ATTACK AND THE GRADUAL ARRIVAL OF BRITISH TROOPS IN THE FIELD

Starting in early 1916, the battalions arriving at the front were mainly drawn from 'Kitchener's Army'. By the summer, these inexperienced but enthusiastic troops constituted more than 60 per cent of the strength of the two armies – the Third and Fourth – that were to attack on 1 July. On that day, it was mainly British troops – English, Scottish, Welsh and Irish – who leaped to the attack rather than troops from the empire. By contrast, large numbers of Canadians, Australians, New Zealanders and South Africans participated in the later stages of the fighting.[36] It must be stressed that, aware that they were participating in a crucial moment of the war, absolutely all of these men were volunteers.

## BUILDING INFRASTRUCTURE

Due to the volume of troops involved, preparing for an offensive on this scale required that massive infrastructural projects be carried out. First and foremost, additional railway lines needed to be constructed and the ballast of existing ones had to be reinforced. Although the troops gathering at the front often travelled there by foot from their positions in the Nord-Pas-de-Calais, their gear, rations and, above all, artillery pieces and ammunition had to be brought by rail. Enormous depots were constructed to house everything necessary for the offensive. Water was also lacking to meet the needs of the nearly 500,000 men and hundreds of thousands of horses gradually converging upon the region. A large number of reservoirs were thus dug and kilometres of pipes laid.

Similarly, large-scale medical infrastructure had to be provided. The first rung consisted of first-aid stations just behind the trench lines. These stations had to supply first aid but were above all meant to perform triage on the influx of wounded men in order to allow the most serious cases to be transferred to the rear as quickly as possible. The circulation of hospital trains was another objective of improving the railway network. General Rawlinson himself asked that, on the day of the attack, at least fourteen trains be made available to his armies to transfer their wounded behind the lines rapidly. In the event, only six were provided... and around fifty needed.

Alongside the large number of wounded who were expected, it was thought that many enemy soldiers would be taken prisoner. The British thus set about constructing barbed-wire enclosures to hold them. Finally, a strange but unfortunately necessary measure in the preparation of any such large-scale offensive: deep pits were dug to provisionally bury the bodies of soldiers who were killed.

Given the large number of troops gathering on the Somme, the soldiers could only stay for brief periods in the trenches from which they were to issue forth on the day of the attack. They thus had to 'rotate' very rapidly to make room for new units, completing their training several kilometres behind the front. In order to prepare for the attack, it was necessary to excavate approach trenches several hundred metres behind the departure trenches so that the troops of the second and third waves could await their turn to attack in relative safety.

Another essential task was to establish telephone-cable networks connecting the trench lines with artillery batteries and command posts. In order to protect them from German fire, the cables had to be buried deeply in narrow trenches. These fixed communications networks thus required the British high command to gather at posts (often located in chateaux) several kilometres behind the front.

By contrast, communications with the attacking troops became very vulnerable and uncertain once they left the departure trenches. It relied on unspooled (but unburied) cables, flares and smoke bombs, messenger pigeons and, above all, runners who, under fire, attempted to cross back and forth across the battlefield in order to maintain contact.

Finally, much energy was spent digging saps towards the German lines. Seven major saps were dug under enemy positions in order to allow mines to be placed there. When set off, their explosions would provide the signal to begin the attack while at the same time destroying the German's forward positions. With the dust hardly settled, the Germans and British would race to be first to take refuge behind the lips of the resultant craters.

## NEW GERMAN FORTIFICATIONS AND THE REINFORCEMENT OF ARTILLERY

Despite efforts on the part of the British to be discreet, the Germans were aware of the work that had begun across from their lines. For the general staff, the question was to determine whether what was being prepared was a major offensive or rather a mere diversion to encourage the German army to reduce its efforts outside Verdun. Over the course of the spring, the local command in any case intensified its fortification efforts and even prepared a third line of trenches. Aware of the growing scale of the British preparations taking place across from them, the infantrymen did not balk at the very heavy work involved in constructing and reinforcing the shelters meant to protect them. In early June, Falkenhayn himself ultimately became convinced of the imminence of a British attack on the Somme and planned to send massive reinforcements. Yet the onset of the Russian offensive in mid-June led him to limit himself to sending two divisions and fifty additional artillery pieces. Set up in the final days of June and neither identified nor spotted by British observers, the latter were to cause much damage on 1 July.

## THE WEEK PRECEDING THE ATTACK

The bombardment of the German positions began on 24 June. It was supposed to last five days, as the infantry attack had originally been planned for the 29th. The British plan of attack included more than 1,400 guns of all calibres, or one artillery piece for every eighteen metres of front line, as well as a vast quantity of ammunition. It was expected that more shells would be fired than had been used by the British artillery over the first twelve months of the war taken together. The early stages of the conflict, it is true, had been marked by chronic insufficiency in shell and ammunition production. Yet the efforts of Lloyd George, Britain's energetic minister of munitions and future prime minister, had begun to pay off. In the course of the week, more than 1.5 million shells would be fired at the German lines. The bombardment continued almost unbroken but with variable intensity over the course of the day.

The densest pounding of artillery began at 6.45 in the morning and lasted twenty-four minutes. At night, half of the guns were left at rest, with the other half periodically firing. At the same time, dense machine-gun fire was concentrated on the German positions to make relieving troops and transporting supplies and materiel difficult. The guns were assigned different tasks depending on their calibre. The field artillery set about destroying the dense barbed-wire networks protecting the German trenches. This was a delicate operation demanding great precision on the part of the artillerymen, particularly in what concerned the adjustment of the shell primers. To be effective, they had to explode at the height of the barbed wire. A fraction of a second too early and the projectile plunged into the soil, where it exploded without destroying the barbed wire, instead digging a crater that rendered the infantry's advance yet more difficult. The heavy artillery targeted the enemy trenches and particularly underground shelters. Deeply buried under narrow trenches, they were difficult to destroy except by direct fire. The artillerymen tried to spot the entries to prevent their use and possibly bury their occupants. Here, too, it was crucial for the artillerymen to have fully mastered their guns. Should they miss their target by just ten metres, which they frequently did at longer ranges, the bombardment was ineffective. Finally, 180 pieces of artillery were assigned to destroy the German artillery positions once they had been located by Allied aviation. These guns, intended for long-range fire, were among the oldest in the British arsenal.

## MILITARY INTELLIGENCE AND TRENCH RAIDS AMONG THE BRITISH AND GERMANS

Both sides conducted regular patrols and raids against the enemy trenches. Doing so served several objectives. First, it helped train troops who otherwise would have passively stood by while contemplating – or being subjected to – bombardment.

Next, it was necessary for the purposes of taking prisoners and identifying the origin and number of enemy forces. Finally and above all, it permitted the soldiers to reconnoitre the terrain and, in the British case, assess the effect of the bombardment: had the barbed wire been cut? Did the German shelters appear to have been destroyed? Depending on the sector and day, British patrolling reports were contradictory. While some claimed that the barbed wire had been almost completely destroyed, most vouched for the fact that it was mainly intact. The Germans, for their part, were also very active. Their objective was to disrupt British preparations and, above all, take prisoners in order to anticipate the date and methods of the forthcoming attack.

## Aerial observation and listening systems

In terms of the number and quality of their aircraft, French and British airmen had a significant advantage over their German adversaries throughout this period on the Somme. While the Germans possessed just 120 aeroplanes, British airmen alone had nearly 200: they could thus operate above enemy positions, a possibility denied their adversaries. Given this asymmetry in the capacity for aerial reconnaissance, the Germans made great efforts to camouflage their aircraft. In order to prevent them from being prematurely located, they kept a large portion of them on the ground until the attack was launched. By contrast, they possessed sophisticated listening networks. This seems to have allowed them to intercept successfully some British telephone communications.

## The operation postponed for forty-eight hours

The attack was initially planned for the morning of 29 July. On the 26th and 27th, however, a series of storms broke out across the region and, on the morning of the 28th, it was still raining.

Since the rain would have further hampered the infantry's advance and, even more so, the job of aerial observation, at eleven in the morning on that day the British command therefore decided to postpone the attack until 1 July. Tense and soaked, tens of thousands of men who had already left their camps for the departure trenches made an about-turn. The bombardment thus continued for two more days. But the shells fired during these two additional days reduced the stockpile available for the day of the attack.

## THE STATE OF MIND IN THE HIGH COMMAND AND AMONG THE TROOPS

Haig and Rawlinson, the British leaders, were convinced that the bombardment had been effective once it was over. Despite the confused reports and cautious observations reaching them from the field, they believed that the infantry would in most cases be able to advance behind the artillery barrage without incident. On the eve of the attack, General Haig made the following note in his journal:

> With God's help, I feel hopeful. The men are in splendid spirits. Several have said that they have never before been so instructed and informed of the nature of the operation before them. The barbed wire has never been so well cut nor the artillery preparation so thorough.[37]

The Fourth Army's commander, Rawlinson, adopted a more measured – indeed, almost fatalistic – tone:

> What the actual result will be, none can say, but I feel pretty confident of success myself, though only after heavy fighting. That the Boche will break and that a débâcle will supervene I do not

believe, but, should this be the case, I am quite ready to take full advantage of it [...] The issues are in the hands of the Bon Dieu.[38]

Subaltern officers and enlisted men had mixed emotions. Those holding front-line trenches could observe that the enemy barbed-wire networks seemed dangerously intact. Many young officers doubted that all of the machine-gun positions facing them had actually been destroyed. That said, all felt part of the conflict's largest concentration of military forces. Above all, the bombardment they witnessed was without historical precedent. The accounts of all survivors mention their amazement at the powerful spectacle that had unfolded before their eyes over the course of the week. Confident in the bombardment's outcome and inspired by the sporting spirit of the English public schools, Captain Wilfred Nevill of the 8th Surrey presented each of his platoon leaders with a football and took bets on who among them would be the first to kick a ball into the German trenches on the day of the attack.

As is often the case, the poets instinctively had a clearer perception of a historic moment that was opaque to contemporaries. William Noel Hodgson (1893–1916) had left Oxford at the declaration of war and immediately enlisted. He debarked in France with the 9th Devonshire on 28 July 1915. One month later, he received the Victoria Cross for exceptional bravery at the Battle of Loos. On the morning of 1 July, he was killed in a German trench he had just captured with his men. Here are the final verses of the poem he wrote on the eve of the attack:

I, that on my familiar hill
Saw with uncomprehending eyes
A hundred of Thy sunsets spill
Their fresh and sanguine sacrifice,
Ere the sun swung his noonday sword

Must say goodbye to all of this!
By all delights that I shall miss,
Help me to die, O Lord.

Fighting on the French side with the Foreign Legion, which he joined in August 1914, the young American poet Alan Seeger wrote a woman friend:

We go up to the attack tomorrow. […] We are to have the honor of marching in the first wave. […] I will write you soon if I get through all right. If not, my only earthly care is for my poems.[39]

After having received his diploma from Harvard in 1912, Seeger left to pursue a romantic and bohemian life in Paris's Latin Quarter. Seeger survived 1 July but was killed three days later on 4 July, American Independence Day. Written in the trenches, his best-known poem is entitled 'I Have a Rendezvous with Death'. These are among his last verses:

I have a rendezvous with Death
At some disputed barricade,
When Spring comes back with rustling shade,
And apple blossoms fill the air.
I have a rendezvous with Death
When Spring brings back blue days and fair…

On the German side, the pressure on the troops crouching in their shelters was very trying. The nearly unbroken bombardment forced them to suspend relief and supplies had run thin over the preceding week. Although the artillery rarely scored direct hits against their shelters, the men were permanently subjected to the physical and psychological pressure of its pounding fire. As one German soldier remarked:

The wait becomes ever more intolerable. The rumbling exhausts, irritates, excites and drives us nearly mad. With strong coffee, strong tea, we keep ourselves awake, calm ourselves, revive ourselves. [...] On several occasions, we thought the shelter was going to collapse under the shock and explosion of a large-calibre shell as it plunged deeply [into the ground]. The shelter seems to give way, the struts already bending. Under the pressure and air current, the gas lamp goes out. Hard, somber, dismal faces: a Passion scene in the trench. Our heads are broken, our strength exhausted, our patience very severely tested. The white of one's eye burns and has gone red. An unhealthy warmth circulates like burning lead in our veins and nervous shudders run through us. We can't stand it any longer.[40]

Even an officer as motivated and experienced as Lieutenant Ernst Jünger crouched at the bottom of his hole:

Occasionally my ears were utterly deafened by a single fiendish crashing burst of flame. Then incessant hissing gave me the sense of hundreds of pound weights rushing down at incredible speed, one after the other. Or a dud shell landed with a short, heavy ground-shaking thump. Shrapnels burst by the dozen, like dainty crackers, shook loose their little balls in a dense cloud, and the empty casings rasped after they were gone. Each time a shell landed anywhere close, the earth flew up and down, and metal shards drove themselves into it. It's an easier matter to describe these sounds than to endure them, because one cannot but associate every single sound of flying steel with the idea of death, and so I huddled in my hole in the ground with my hand in front of my face, imagining all the possible variants of being hit.[41]

Some soldiers broke down and went mad. The resilience of the immense majority of them is only more remarkable for that: indeed, most of the positions continued to be held until the start of the attack. It was only against the French troops, who they strongly doubted would participate in the British offensive, that the Germans sometimes evacuated their front line and withdrew to secondary positions, with orders to rush forward to reoccupy them as soon as the attack got under way.

### THE EVE OF THE ATTACK AND THE FINAL PREPARATIONS

When night finally fell around 10 p.m. on the evening of the 30th, the British troops set off towards their departure trenches. The accounts of survivors underscore the mixture of enthusiasm and real anxiety they felt.[42] Most of these men had yet to see combat; that such a corrosive wait was finally coming to an end came as a relief.

Having reached the departure positions, their last meal arrived before dawn with their coffee canteens, to which generous quantities of rum had been added.

At 4 a.m., the men learned that the attack would not take place just before sunrise as they had expected but rather at 7.30 and thus in full sunlight. Most found the news worrisome, particularly given that the barbed-wire networks opposite them seemed on the whole intact.

At many places along the front, the Germans launched a violent pre-emptive bombardment around 5.30. All of the batteries that had kept quiet over the preceding days to avoid identification entered into action. Face down in their shallow departure trenches, the British chalked up large casualties:

even before the attack had begun, the first wounded men were flooding back to the aid stations. The officers synchronized their watches and had cases of grenades opened and their contents distributed to the men. As with every morning for seven days, at 6.25 the British artillery began a massive bombardment. The nearly Wagnerian spectacle of the deluge of shells crashing down on the German positions made a major impression on the British soldiers massed on the parapets and somewhat reassured them.

In a staccato of short sentences, the English poet Siegfried Sassoon noted his impressions in his journal from his trench outside Fricourt:

> Saty. July 1st, 1916, 7.30 a.m. Last night was cloudless & starry & still – the bombardment went on steadily. We had breakfast at 6 – the morning is brilliant fine – after a mist early. Since 6.30 there has been hell let loose. The air vibrates with the incessant din – the whole earth shakes & rocks & throbs. It is one continuous roar – machine guns tap & rattle – bullets whistling overhead – small fry quite outdone by the gangs of hooligan shells that dash over to reach the German lines with their demolition parties. The smoke-cloud is cancelled as the wind is wrong since yesterday. Attack should be starting now but one can't look out because the machine-gun bullets are skimming. Inferno – inferno – bang – smash!![43]

The mines were set to explode at 7.28, or two minutes before the infantry launched its assault: it was hoped that this would deny the German defenders, thus alerted by the mines' detonation, the time needed to dash from their shelters and race to their firing positions. An exception was oddly made for the mine placed under what the British had baptized Hawthorn Ridge outside Beaumont-Hamel. The commander of the infantry brigade that was to carry out the attack had insisted that it be prematurely detonated at 7.20 in order to give his men a chance to rush forward and take up positions on the crater's lip. They did not make it.

At 7.30, British officers sounded their whistles and the first men leaped over the parapets. From his departure trench outside Montauban-de-Picardie, Captain Nevill hurled his football into no man's land, jumped over the parapet and rushed forward with his men.

# CHAPTER 10

## 1 JULY 1916: THE FIRST HOUR

The precise circumstances of the attack varied from one unit to another, with their assaults experiencing diverse outcomes. Yet its progress everywhere observed the same stages.

### THE INITIAL ASSAULT

At 7.30, the British and German bombardments almost simultaneously halted. The sound of the officers' whistles resonated all the louder in the trenches. The British artillerymen prepared to extend their battery fire to the German second-line trenches. Their German counterparts, by contrast, prepared to shorten theirs. After having targeted the British approach and departure trenches, they would now concentrate their fire on no man's land. Following their platoon leaders, the British soldiers crossed one after the other over their trench parapets – a tricky undertaking that involved climbing several steps up a rudimentary ladder while carrying a kit weighing 30 kilograms or more (water, dressing, grenades and, above all, ammunition for the forthcoming hours of combat). From this point on, the soldiers began to fall. The departure trenches were on average located a little more than 400 metres from the German front line, or very much in the range of machine guns, which almost immediately began to wreak havoc.

The initial advance of British troops was immediately slowed by the need to clear the first barbed-wire network: one intended to protect the British trenches from German assault. Openings had of course been cut in advance, but they actually had the effect of concentrating the movement of troops in a limited number of places. Above all, these passages were sometimes prepared a day or two ahead of time and marked with pieces of highly visible white tissue. When the German machine-gunners succeeded in laying their fire down on these points of passage, its impact was particularly lethal.

Once the first line of barbed wire had been crossed, the British troops for the most part deployed in regular lines, as they had been instructed to do. They marched in step, their bodies upright. This choice of a rigid and exposed formation, slowly advancing toward the enemy trenches rather than rushing to attack them, was greeted with disbelief by the German soldiers, who were surprised to have been offered such easy targets. Of course, marching in step also significantly increased the time necessary to cross no man's land.

The British soldiers rapidly found themselves confronted with a new network of barbed wire, that of the Germans. This time, however, the attackers were not only exposed to very close-range machine-gun fire but also to the dense rifle fire of all of the German soldiers who had taken up their stations on the fire step. The condition of the German barbed wire varied. In a small number of cases, it had actually been destroyed or almost destroyed by the preliminary bombardment. In others, the bombardment had merely shifted its position by throwing it into the air, from which it fell in nearly impassable hedges. In most cases, it was simply intact. British sappers did their best to cut openings but, once again, this had the effect of supplying the German machine guns with targets for concentrated fire, now at very close range.

Having reached the barbed wire, the attackers could at least attempt to fire upon their adversaries and riposte with their rifles or grenades. Here and there, first-wave attackers succeeded in gaining a foothold in the German front line. Sometimes they had been abandoned by their defenders, who had fallen back towards the reserve trenches when they saw the attackers – or what was left of them – clear the barbed-wire networks as best they could. Sometimes their adversaries were waiting for the British soldiers with their hands in the air, surrendering or attempting to do so. In most cases, however, brief and very violent hand-to-hand fighting took place. At this stage of the battle, neither side took many prisoners.

The British troops who succeeded in gaining a foothold in a front-line German trench or part of one were immediately confronted with the matter of consolidating their position. The German bombardment had resumed, however, and was now concentrated on no man's land. It sought to impede further the advance of the second and third assault waves, and as far as possible to prevent the most advanced British troops from resupplying or communicating with the rear. The first-wave units suffered appalling losses in killed and wounded. The surviving officers, when there were any, had to consider how they were to hold their positions with the fraction of able-bodied troops remaining to them while at the same time trying to care for the wounded, who were very difficult to evacuate under fire.

For a portion of first-wave units, the explicit mission consisted of immediately pushing beyond the German front line (which was supposed to be taken within a few minutes) to the second. The officers responsible for these groups thus had to decide whether they still had enough men to continue their advance. They also had to try to get an idea of the progress made by the units located to their right and left. If the latter had been turned back, advancing further would risk exposing them to a flanking attack and thus to the possibility of being encircled, captured or killed.

In most cases, these decisions had to be made without the benefit of communications with the rear. The coils of telephone wire had often not been unspooled since the soldiers responsible for doing so had been put out of action. When the wire had been laid, it was regularly cut by explosions. No one could expose themselves for the time necessary to transmit messages by flags. English flares mixed with those of the Germans, creating formidable problems of interpretation. In order to communicate with the rear, the British troops thus mainly relied on runners, who attempted – for the most part unsuccessfully – to cross the battlefield, first in one direction and then the other. The German bombardment was particularly dense and accurate in no man's land, since the German gunners had had plenty of time to identify and set the firing coordinates necessary for great accuracy.

Very often, the soldiers who had successfully penetrated the German trenches were now reduced to small groups of men led by NCOs or particularly determined enlisted men. These were the men who had to choose – sometimes for their group, sometimes individually – between continuing their advance, digging in in anticipation of the inevitable German counter-attack or even evacuating the positions they had just conquered (and at what a price!) in order to rejoin the main body of British troops, which had been brought to a standstill by enemy fire a few hundred metres to the rear.

Overall, the situation was as follows: along the front's southern extremity, the attack had proven relatively successful, with the troops benefiting from very effective cover by French artillery; in the centre, where the British general staff had hoped for a breakthrough, the attackers instead suffered massive defeats; and, in the north, the diversionary operation in which Third Army units were engaged met with near-total failure.

To the south of the British operation, the French attack unfolded almost exactly as the British had hoped theirs would. Adjoining the British army, the artillery of the French 20th Corps actually destroyed most of the fortifications of the Germans' first two lines. It had also nearly everywhere destroyed their barbed wire. At this stage of the conflict, French artillerymen were, it is true, much more experienced than their British counterparts. Moreover, they possessed twice as many heavy artillery pieces (900 versus 460) for a front half as wide. Persuaded that the French would only play a diversionary role on the Somme, finally, the Germans had not taken the same care in preparing their defences as they did before the British. By attacking in small groups of men who rushed forward, the French troops had rapidly reached the first line of German trenches with a minimum of casualties.

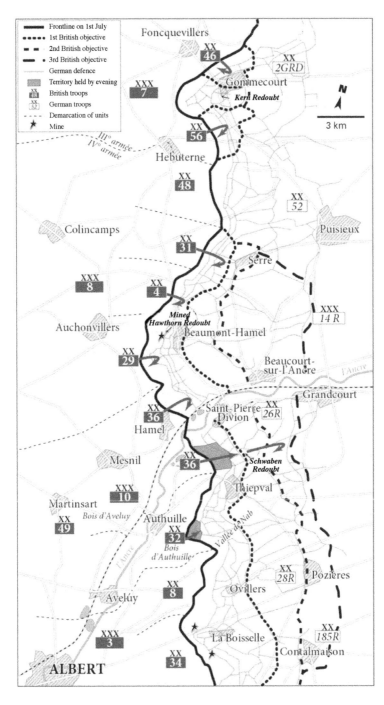

**NORTHWARD MOVEMENT OF THE FRONT: 1 JULY 1916**

In the south, the British operation's three divisions (the 30th, 18th and 7th) thus achieved their objective: to take the first two trench lines.[44] The soldiers of the Manchester Battalion had linked up with the first French troops of the 20th Corps and were headed for the village of Montauban, their objective for the day. The units of the 7th Division also advanced, though less rapidly and with higher casualties. They were stopped outside their objective (the fortified ruins of the village of Mametz) and waited for a new bombardment before attempting to take it. Outside Fricourt, by contrast, the men of the 21st Division had taken a foothold in some parts of the Germans' front-line trenches but seemed incapable of advancing further.

The centre of the British Fourth Army operation was critical to the success of the offensive. It was there, between Thiepval and La Boisselle, that Haig hoped to punch enough of a hole in the German front to allow his cavalry to be unleashed for a breakthrough near Pozières. Five divisions (the 3rd, 8th, 34th, 36th and, in reserve, 49th) were deployed along an eight-kilometre front. They were distributed on both sides of a straight road running nearly perpendicular to the front line from Albert to Bapaume.[45] The German positions had been set up in La Boisselle and Ovillers on hills overlooking two valleys upon which British maps had conferred the unpoetic names of 'Sausage' and 'Mash'. Apart from a handful of (costly) successes, like that of the 34th Division's Glasgow Commercials,[46] British troops were repelled with heavy casualties. The British exploded two major mines in this sector at 7.28 ('Y Sap' and 'Lochnagar').[47]

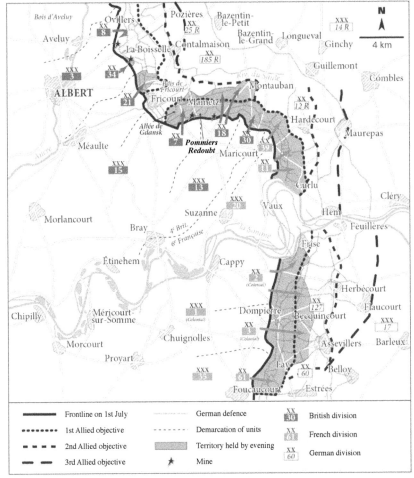

| | | | |
|---|---|---|---|
| —— Frontline on 1st July | ·········· German defence | **XX** 30 | British division |
| •••••• 1st Allied objective | - - - - - Demarcation of units | **XX** 61 | French division |
| ▬ ▬ ▬ 2nd Allied objective | ░░ Territory held by evening | **XX** 60 | German division |
| ▬ ▬ 3rd Allied objective | ⋆ Mine | | |

**SOUTHWARD MOVEMENT OF THE FRONT: 1 JULY 1916**

The units to the north of the Fourth Army operation had varying luck. In the midst of a series of generalized failures, the 36th Division (the Ulster Division, which consisted of Protestant soldiers, some of whom went into battle wearing the sash of the Orange Order) met with unexpected success outside Thiepval but found itself dangerously isolated. Its men succeeded in deeply penetrating German lines but over a narrow front as the units to their left and right had been repelled. They continued to advance vigorously northward, but as they did so the risk that they would be cut off from the rest of the British troops grew. For neither the troops of the 29th Division (on their left) nor those of the 32nd Division (on their right) had succeeded in reaching the first German trenches.

The units of the British Third Army, finally, found themselves outside the village of Gommecourt, at the northern edge of the operation. As the offensive was conceived, these territorial units had been assigned a diversionary role. They were to cover the left flank of the Fourth Army, which was responsible for carrying out the planned breakthrough. Fundamentally, their role was to attract German fire in order to facilitate the job of the Fourth Army further to the south.[48] From this point of view – and only from this point of view – a cynic might see this part of the operation as having been a success. Although one of the two divisions sent into battle, the 56th (or London Territorials), courageously achieved a large part of its objectives and nearly reached Gommecourt, the units of the British Third Army suffered heavy casualties. By contrast, the division with which it was sent into battle, the Midlands Division, met with bloody failure.

## THE SITUATION AT 8.30 IN THE MORNING

An hour after the offensive had been launched, the situation was as follows:

Sixty-six thousand men distributed among 84 regiments had gone into battle as part of the first wave. In sixty minutes, around 30,000 of them had been killed, wounded or taken prisoner – or half of all losses for the day. From this point on, it was clear, at least to observers with a direct view of the battlefield, that the preliminary bombardment had failed to destroy the German defences as expected. On the contrary, the enemy was able to bring sustained fire to bear on the British troops.

At 8.30, forty-three additional regiments already assembled in the approach trenches were in their turn expected to join the assault over the course of the morning. Seventy additional battalions were held in reserve at the command's disposition to intervene where necessary.

At this point, the question was whether or not to pursue the offensive: should the units already assembled in the approach trenches be sent into battle?

With the benefit of a century's hindsight, an observer acquainted with the day's events may find the answer obvious. The preliminary condition for the attack's success – that is, the destruction of the defensive capacity of the German front line – had clearly not been achieved. At this specific point in the day, however, it must be acknowledged that neither the British commander in chief, Haig, at his headquarters at Beauquesne Chateau, nor the commander of the Fourth Army, Rawlinson, at that of Querrieu, was in a position to reach a reasoned decision. The information making its way to them from the fifteen adjacent battlefields between Gommecourt and Montauban was simply too fragmentary, scattered, incomplete and often contradictory. For the remainder of the day, Haig and Rawlinson were to remain nearly totally incapable of obtaining an accurate and trustworthy view of the development of fighting and the progress made by their troops. Responsibility for deciding whether new units should be sent into battle thus fell to their subordinates, the corps and divisional commanders closer to the field. These men reached their decisions in keeping with local circumstances but also as disciplined officers who desired as far as possible to stick to the plan of attack that had been imparted by their leaders.

At 8.30, General de Beauvoir de Lisle, commander of the 29th Division, thus received a message that a white flare had been spotted from the trench attacked by the 1st Royal Inniskilling Fusiliers outside Beaumont-Hamel. In fact, it was a German flare requesting that the artillery extend its fire. Beauvoir de Lisle, however, interpreted it as a message from the Scottish soldiers of the first wave indicating that they had taken the enemy trench. At 8.45, he thus ordered the Newfoundland Regiment to move forward to pursue and build upon the (supposed) Scottish advance. At 9.15, its soldiers thus began marching forward. Nearly 90 per cent of them would not return.

# CHAPTER 11

## 1 JULY 1916: THE REST OF THE DAY

As we have seen, the decision as to whether to launch new attacks over the course of the morning was thus not taken by army commanders such as Rawlinson or Lieutenant General Edmund Allenby, commander of the Third Army. Like Haig, they were too far from the front to get a quick and accurate idea of what was a confused and evolving situation. While more than 30,000 of his soldiers and officers had in fact already been killed or wounded, that morning Haig noted in his journal: 'Along a front of more than twenty-four kilometres, one can expect uneven results.' At the time, the author of these lines was still unaware of the extent to which the premise of that day's attack had been proven false. In fact, the bombardment of German positions had not destroyed their capacity to defend themselves against the infantry's advance. But neither Rawlinson nor Allenby, much less Haig, was capable of discerning it from their command posts in the rear. Throughout the day, the reports that made their way to them were belated, incomplete and often mistaken. What's more, the bureaucratic phenomenon by which bad news only slowly and partially moves up the chain of command while good news travels quickly, being amplified as it goes, was fully at work throughout the day. The decision to send new assault waves was thus mainly taken by divisional and army corps (two divisions) commanders. At the time, military leaders were mainly judged on the basis of their drive and certainly not on their ability to economize men. In most cases, the unsuccessful assaults of the first hour were thus briskly renewed.

The soldiers who threw themselves into battle at 7.30 could not help but feel apprehension regarding the uncertain fate that awaited them. For those who were to attack later in the morning, unfortunately, that uncertainty had largely faded. From their approach trenches, they were able to get the measure of the intensity of German fire and were subjected to the effects of bombardment. As they advanced towards their departure trenches along the communication saps, they encountered the unstinting flow of wounded men heading back to the rear, some covered in blood but moving on their own, others carried on stretchers or a comrade's shoulders. It was in any case an impressive spectacle, particularly for those soldiers – the majority – who were to have their baptism of fire on that day.

In the north of the British operation, the role of the Third Army, as we have seen, was to create a diversion to draw away a disproportionate share of German troops and fire. At the tactical level, its objective was to carry out a pincer movement around the village of Gommecourt with two divisions of territorials, the North Midlands to the north and the London Territorials to the south. Over the course of the initial assault, the Midlands soldiers were pushed back with heavy casualties while elements of the London Territorials succeeded in clearing several lines of trenches, deeply penetrating the enemy defences and approaching Gommecourt. Given that the British plan did not provide for advancing beyond Gommecourt should the village be taken and had already achieved its diversionary purpose, it might have seemed reasonable for General Thomas Snow, the commander of these two divisions, to content himself with consolidating their positions. Oddly, however, he chose to resume the attack of the North Midlands Division – already sorely tried earlier that morning – rather than reinforce the positions where his soldiers had succeeded in advancing. The new attack had the same calamitous result as its predecessor. Once the Midlands soldiers had been definitively pushed back, the German defenders were able gradually to concentrate their fire and efforts on the London Territorial soldiers. Exhausted and isolated, the latter were little by little forced to abandon their positions, first the most advanced and then nearly all of them. After heavy casualties, by day's end they had virtually returned to their departure lines.

In the north and centre of the Fourth Army's operation, the repeated attacks of the morning almost all ended in failure. The only exception was between Thiepval and the river Ancre, where the advance of the 36th Division (the 'Ulster Division') met with unexpected success. The Northern Irish soldiers[49] were among those who had been able to prepare for the initial assault by moving closer to German lines, using for cover a small copse that still stood in no man's land outside Thiepval. Less exposed to machine-gun fire, they were able rapidly to penetrate the German trenches before their defenders were in position. The division's six regiments then immediately pressed on towards a German fortification known as the 'Schwaben [Swabian] Redoubt', taking control of it that morning after extremely violent fighting. Reinforced by two additional regiments of soldiers from Belfast, the Ulstermen then attempted to push forward towards Grandcourt. As the day moved on, however, the men grew exhausted from the unbroken hours of combat. Above all, their advance within German lines had gradually isolated them from the rest of the British operation. Reserves and ammunition dwindled. As the hours passed, German counter-attacks became more frequent and pressing. Additional reinforcements were requested to relieve the exhausted units but never came. Little by little, the Ulstermen retreated, first across the Schwaben Redoubt and then, at twilight, towards what had been the first German trenches at dawn that morning. There, they encountered the soldiers of the West Yorkshire Reserve Division, who had finally arrived to reinforce them, though too late to allow them to hold the Schwaben Redoubt, which was only to be retaken by British troops three months later. On that night, the Orangemen handed the 800 metres of German trench they had conquered over to the relief troops. They set off for the rear to dress their wounds, but without that day's 2,000 dead, 2,700 wounded and 165 prisoners.

The bloody assault of the Newfoundland soldiers outside Beaumont-Hamel has already been recounted. It resulted in the loss of more than 90 per cent of the regiment's strength, with most of those who fell having been hit in the open field before they even reached their departure trenches. It should be mentioned that another unit, the Essex Regiment, was to attack the German positions at the same time as the Newfoundlanders. Its commander, however, chose to move his troops forward in the relative safety of the communication trenches, although they were obstructed with the dead, the wounded and various other obstacles. It thus took the Essex soldiers two hours to cross 300 metres and reach their departure trenches. From there, they rushed forward but were repelled without encountering any opposition. They were no more able to approach the German trenches than were the Newfoundlander soldiers. But their casualties were limited (if one may put it thus) to only 30 per cent of their strength.

At the centre of the Fourth Army's operation between Ovillers and La Boisselle, the 8th and 34th divisions spent the morning attempting to advance along what the British maps dubbed the 'Mash' and 'Sausage' valleys. The layout of the terrain, where the Germans held the commanding positions, and the concentration of German artillery guns resulted in the failure of successive British attempts. While the 8th Division mainly consisted of veterans, the 34th was made up of recent volunteers. Their fate was the same. As the price for its efforts, the 8th Division lost more than 5,000 men killed or wounded over the course of the day, and the 34th would be the most sorely tested of all British divisions, with casualties totalling more than 6,500 men. For Haig and Rawlinson, the utter failure at the centre of their operation was particularly critical as it was here that they counted on breaking through the German front and possibly bringing up the two divisions of cavalry waiting several kilometres behind the lines. This failure partly paralysed their ability to exploit more unexpected successes.

As mentioned above, the only real British successes of the day were had on the right wing of General Rawlinson's Fourth Army. From the start of the attack, the 30th Division, which adjoined the French Sixth Army and partly profited from its heavy artillery cover, rapidly advanced through successive German lines of defence. At morning's end, it took its designated objective for the day, the village of Montauban-de-Picardie. Of the thirteen British divisions sent into battle that morning, it alone achieved all of its objectives.

The 7th Division, for its part, advanced more slowly

towards its objective, the village of Mametz, which was heavily defended by the Germans but fell to the attackers in the early afternoon. Located between the other two, the 18th Division also advanced. By mid-afternoon, the British troops had been able to secure deep control over a nearly five-kilometre front.

Since the French troops operating on their right had achieved a similar breakthrough, the German lines now presented a nearly ten-kilometre gap that could be opened and through which the British cavalry could have swept before the Germans rallied and sent reinforcements to plug it. This opportunity – the only one of the day – was not seized upon by General Rawlinson.

Despite the danger and the explosion of the mines, the start of the attack certainly came as something of a relief to a large number of German soldiers: they would finally be able to leave their continually bombarded shelters and defend themselves in open air! For the German troops facing the Third Army and the northern and central portions of the Fourth Army, the day – bloody and nerve-racking, to be sure – was on the whole ultimately rather favourable. In most cases, the shelters and barbed-wire networks protecting them had not been destroyed. Most often alerted by the end of the bombardment ten minutes before the attack, these men were able to reach their firing positions before the British had advanced deeply into no man's land. It was with joy, finally, that they watched as their adversaries approached, marching in line, a formation that particularly exposed them to machine-gun and rifle fire from the trenches and the artillery's barrage.

Noting his surprise and satisfaction faced with these British tactics, one German soldier wrote:

> When the English started advancing we were very worried; they looked as though they must

overrun our trenches. We were very surprised to see them walking, we had never seen that before. [...] When we started firing, we just had to load and reload. They went down in their hundreds. You didn't have to aim, we just fired into them. If only they had run, they would have overwhelmed us.[50]

Where the British soldiers had been able to penetrate enemy lines, German tactical flexibility and the sense of initiative of their NCOs had allowed them to launch very rapidly what were often decisive counter-attacks. In particular, the only breach north of Albert that really worried the German command – the 36th Ulster Division's breakthrough north of Thiepval – had been plugged late in the day with the recapture of the Schwaben Redoubt.

By contrast, the situation of the German army was completely different to the south of the British Fourth Army and, above all, the French Sixth Army. There, the preliminary bombardment had indeed succeeded in dismantling the German entrenchments and destroying the barbed-wire networks. Casualties were high and many trenches had been abandoned before the attack. By providing cover for the British 30th Division and allowing it to advance towards and subsequently take the village of Montauban, the effective French bombardment had a domino effect. The advance of the 30th Division on their left had then forced the German defenders of Mametz to withdraw faced with the assaults of the 7th and 18th divisions. By late afternoon, the situation had become critical for the Germans in this sector. General von Stein had evacuated his headquarters in Bapaume, which he believed to be threatened. Lacking available reinforcements, all able-bodied men – cooks, grooms and postmen – were issued rifles and rushed to the line. At this moment, the German general staff felt it was on a razor's edge.

Rawlinson nevertheless refused his subordinates' requests to profit from the long summer's day to move up the reserve infantry and, above all, the Indian cavalry division, which had been waiting since early morning. But he had every reason not to listen to them. Besides, in late morning he had already informed the cavalry units that they would not be taking part in the battle that day after all.

Rawlinson was an infantry officer with little respect for what he saw as the romantic myth of the cavalry breakthrough. He intended to apply his personal doctrine: 'Bite and hold.' He thus wanted to consolidate the day's gains over the positions that had been won, move the artillery forward overnight, resume the bombardment, move his infantry forward again, and so on. What's more, on this 1 July afternoon he was hardly inclined to take a decisive strategic decision on the basis of information received from the field. For most of the morning, the messages that made their way to him from the other sectors of the front had been positive and optimistic before rapidly deteriorating as the hours passed. There was thus no way of knowing whether the reports he was receiving from his right wing really were more reliable. He was told that the first enemy lines had been taken and that, behind them, the German army seemed absent from this area of the front. Yet everywhere else where the British had initially made progress, the Germans had rapidly counter-attacked in strength. Finally, the idea of becoming involved in a breakthrough attempt the success of which would in large measure depend upon collaboration with the French army hardly filled him with enthusiasm. In contrast with Haig, he did not especially respect his French counterparts.

To the right of the British Fourth Army, French troops

also made very rapid progress and with a minimum of casualties. By noon, General Maurice Balfourier's 20th Corps had reached all of its objectives for the day. South of the Somme, the Colonial Corps and the 25th Corps, which began their advance at 9.30, saw that the first two German lines had been virtually destroyed by the bombardment and that German troops seemed to have largely evacuated their positions before the bombardment had even ended. The road to Péronne seemed open. But when the French liaison officers present at Rawlinson's headquarters reported that the latter had decided not to advance, the French commander halted his troops in his turn. There was no question of the French army advancing alone if the British troops on its left flank did not do so, for that would be to expose the Sixth Army to German counter-attack. Above all, for French military leaders, obliging their British ally to participate massively in land operations on the Western Front was a fundamental objective of the Battle of the Somme. There was no question of advancing without the British while allowing them to halt on the evening of the offensive's first day.

# CHAPTER 12

## 1 JULY 1916: DEAD AND WOUNDED

From the outset, it must be emphasized that this accounting is difficult to establish with precision. For one must first distinguish between figures for the dead and those for the larger, more indistinct category of 'casualties'. Casualty figures include the dead, the wounded, the missing and those taken prisoner. Obviously, the manner in which they are distributed is susceptible to evolution over time: the wounded will die, the missing will reappear, either alive and in the form of prisoners or, sometimes long afterwards, as corpses. Much also depends on the rigour with which casualties were counted locally, something that varied from one army and period of the conflict to the next. Where the British were particularly meticulous, the Germans were less so, only reporting their figures roughly once every ten days. Before considering the figures in detail, in short, it is important to be aware that they contain almost insurmountable areas of uncertainty, even when they are presented by official sources at the level of each unit.

Nevertheless, even when all necessary precautions are

taken with regards to the accuracy of these figures, it is clear that 1 July 1916 was quite simply the bloodiest day in all of British history.

To take its full measure, it is absolutely necessary to consider in detail the gruesome bookkeeping of the official total of British casualties for the day, or 57,470 men:

Killed: 19,240, including 993 officers
Wounded: 35,493, including 1,337 officers
Missing: 2,152, including 96 officers
Prisoners: 585, including 12 officers
Total: 57,470, including 2,438 officers

If one allows that the missing were killed but in circumstances that did not allow their remains to be identified – they had been buried or directly hit by a shell, for example – more than 21,000 British soldiers died on this day.

Published in 1971, Martin Middlebrook's classic work on the first day of the Battle of the Somme[51] offers a fascinating analysis of the breakdown of casualties. It is worth recalling in detail. First of all, the total number of those killed on that day may be compared to that for other bloody events in the history of the British army. The one-day Battle of Waterloo resulted in 8,500 casualties. Combined casualties for British and Canadian forces in the course of the D-Day landings on 6 June 1944 were 4,000 men. At El Alamein, the British lost a daily average of 1,100 men for eleven days. Another way of describing total casualties is to note that it is greater than the combined total of British casualties for the Crimean War, the conflict against the Boers and the intervention in Korea.

If one considers the casualty figures for 1 July in themselves, one may make the following observations. On that day, a total of 120,000 men distributed among 143 regiments went into battle, 60,000 of them in the attack's first wave. Almost exactly half of them were killed, wounded or taken prisoner. Among officers, the casualty rate reached 75 per cent. The hierarchical rank with the highest casualty rate was that of captain – that is, the highest-ranking officer likely to lead his men personally into battle as a company commander.[52]

Casualties were of course concentrated in the infantry. Out of the total of 57,450 men, one finds 170 artillerymen, sixty doctors and nurses, and five airmen, but apparently no cavalrymen. In the infantry, by contrast, casualties could vary twofold from one division to another: from 3,000 or fewer for the 30th Division, which took Montauban, to 6,000 or more for the 34th and 29th divisions (to which the Newfoundland Regiment belonged). The amount of time spent advancing across no man's land without cover seems to explain these disparities.

At the regimental level, the highest casualty rate was that of the Newfoundland Regiment but the highest absolute total was that of the 10th Regiment of the 34th Division (West Yorkshire), which lost 751 men outside Fricourt after having spent most of the day pinned down by intense machine-gun fire between the first and second German lines.

As mentioned above, the majority of troops sent into battle on 1 July were drawn from the new army – Kitchener's Army – with many regiments consisting of 'pals battalions' recruited by locality. The consequence of this geographical concentration of recruits was a corresponding concentration of casualties. Around mid-July, a number of English localities were overwhelmed by the arrival of thousands of letters bearing grim news from the War Office.

Ironically, the battle itself, during which these pals battalions won such renown under fire, was to undermine their particular nature. Decimated units were reinforced and rebuilt with new recruits from across England. Though they retained their names, all of these units would over the course of the remaining years of the war lose their original regional character.

On the French side, the day's favourable developments limited casualties, at least in comparison with those suffered by the British. Total casualties for the day were around 1,500 men, a reflection of the fact that, on the front assigned the French army, the fighting that day had gone as planned: effective bombardment destroyed the front line and allowed the men to advance with relative ease. The fighting that followed was nevertheless to prove much more costly for the French army.

Lacking daily tallies of troop strength comparable to those meticulously prepared by the British, casualties among the German army troops who faced them are much more difficult to evaluate. By extrapolating from samples, however, their total number of casualties can be estimated as at between 8,000 and 10,000 men, including 2,000 prisoners.

## TREATING THE WOUNDED

Despite the historical record of the number killed, most of the day's casualties consisted of wounded soldiers. A number of remarks need to be made about the manner in which they were processed. Obviously, the methodical preparations for the offensive took account of the large number of wounded that would result as well as the structured chain of care that would be necessary to deal with them. Yet the particular circumstances in which the fighting took place and above all the unexpectedly high number of cases requiring attention seriously disrupted aid operations and contributed to further increasing the total number of dead.

The first problem was to retrieve the wounded. Most of them lay in no man's land: their evacuation by stretcher-bearers was disrupted by the Germans' incessant fire to prevent reinforcement. In many places, what's more, British forces had succeeded in achieving territorial gains but had to abandon them before the day's end. As a result, British wounded sometimes found themselves spread around areas that were no longer under their comrades' control. When night came, there was only sporadic and uneven cooperation between British and Germans to find the dead and wounded. In some sectors, a formal ceasefire was reached between opposing units and was more or less respected. In others, there was no ceasefire, even tacit. In some cases, wounded soldiers were found after having been run through by bayonet or with their heads smashed, suggesting that they had been finished off by German patrols. Finally, stretcher-bearers – and stretchers – were in short supply. Throughout the day, cooks, artillerymen and radio operators were called upon to search for the wounded together with anything that could be in one way or another used to transport them (boards, blankets and so on).

Throughout the evening and the night that followed, wounded soldiers crawled towards the British lines. Others reappeared over the course of the following days. The most extreme case was that of a Third Army soldier found lying paralysed but still alive outside Gommecourt two weeks after the offensive – the shell hole in which he had been lying was partly filled with water, allowing him to slake his thirst. However, most of those not rapidly retrieved died on the spot from their wounds, often from a combination of shock and haemorrhage.

The account of James McGrath, a soldier in the Newfoundland Regiment, provides a good idea of the ordeal of wounded men in no man's land as they attempted to make their way back to their lines:

The Germans actually mowed us down like sheep.

I managed to get to their barbed wire, where I got the first shot. Then [when I] went to jump into their trench, I got the second in the leg.

I lay in No Man's Land for fifteen hours, and then crawled a distance of a mile and a quarter. They fired on me again, this time fetching me in the left leg [...] So I waited for another hour, and moved again, only having the use of my left arm now.

As I was doing splendidly, nearing our own trench, they again fetched me, this time around the hip as I crawled on. I managed to get to our own line, which I saw was evacuated as our artillery was playing heavily on their trenches. They retaliated, and kept me in a hole for another hour.

Only then was I rescued by Captain Windeler, who took me on his back to the dressing station, a distance of two miles.[53]

Moreover, the front-line trenches were themselves rapidly obstructed with wounded waiting to be evacuated as well as the bodies of those who had made it back to their trench before succumbing to their wounds. The need to remove these corpses very rapidly became a major sanitary and even military problem.

The first stage in evacuating the wounded generally consisted of a battalion first-aid post located in the reserve trench. There, the doctor assigned to the regiment endeavoured to treat the most serious cases of haemorrhage while letting through those capable of surviving a somewhat longer trip to the rear.

The dressing station, often just out of range of German fire, was the next stage. No surgery took place there, either, but ambulance personnel attempted to dress the most serious wounds in order to reduce the risk of infection and above all to allow the evacuation to Casualty Clearing Stations to continue. The wounded were (in principle) conveyed to these stations, located around fifteen kilometres behind the front, by a constantly rotating fleet of motorized ambulances.

At the Casualty Clearing Stations, surgery was performed on the soldiers. The hospitals of the Fourth Army, however, could only treat 10,000 wounded at a time and, on that day, three times that number arrived. These field hospitals had been set up along just-constructed rail lines in order to dispatch as many of the wounded as possible to hospitals behind the lines, some of them as far away as England. Rawlinson, commander of the Fourth Army, had asked that fourteen hospital trains be ready to evacuate its wounded on the day of the attack. In the event, only five were made available to him on 1 July – three in the morning and two in the evening. They evacuated a total of 3,127 men, the majority of whom had fallen ill or been wounded in the days leading up to the battle. For days on end, tens of thousands of wounded men would wait for the arrival of additional trains allowing them to be evacuated – with predictable consequences.

All things considered, the fate of the wounded on this day varied widely. Most often, it depended on the place and time that they were wounded as well as the severity of the wounds themselves. A small number of the wounded had the luck of ending their day in a hospital bed in England. A much larger number spent the next several days dying in the shell holes of no man's land.

# CHAPTER 13

## WHY DID 1 JULY 1916 END IN DEFEAT?

Could the disaster that befell the British army that day have been predicted? Could it have been avoided?

With the luxury of nearly a century's hindsight, it is clear that the fundamental premise of the British battle plan – the notion that a long and massive bombardment might entirely crush the enemy's ability to resist the infantry's advance – was false, at least at this stage of the conflict. A number of factors explain the relative ineffectiveness of British artillery, particularly in comparison with that of the French.

### THE DENSITY OF BOMBARDMENT WAS INSUFFICIENT

A total of 1,500 guns took part in the British bombardment preceding the Somme attack, firing 1.5 million shells over the course of a week. At the time, these seemed like astronomical figures. In July 1917, however – that is, just one year later – British artillerymen loosed 4.5 million shells on the German positions at Passchendaele (western Flanders). In a chapter devoted to the Battle of the Somme in his now classic work, *The Face of Battle*, John Keegan showed convincingly that, in contrast to the French, whose bombardment was indisputably more effective, the density of British fire was insufficient given the breadth of the front and the number of objectives that had been earmarked for destruction.[54] The French artillery used almost the same number of guns as their British counterparts (1,400 vs 1,500) but against a front that was only half as wide. Moreover, the better part of French artillery consisted of heavy guns. Little surprise, then, that the French bombardment should have been more effective.

## THE INEXPERIENCE AND INACCURACY OF BRITISH GUNNERS

For artillerymen located several kilometres from their target, hitting a trench line into which shelters have been dug requires great precision. A trench line is by definition narrow: a shot that misses the target by ten metres in either direction will have practically no effect. To destroy a concrete shelter buried ten metres beneath the trench virtually requires a direct hit (a very exceptional event). Sighting in long-distance artillery demands great experience on the part of gunners. At this stage of the war, however, British artillerymen[55] lacked the know-how that would be theirs in 1917 and 1918. For example, the metal barrel of a gun that fires hundreds of shells without interruption will slightly expand as it heats. A 75-mm gun might thus end the day with a diameter of 77 mm or more. Since the diameter of the shells it fires remains unchanged at 75 mm, their trajectory will be affected. The gunner must thus know how to compensate for this.

## TOO MANY FRAGMENTATION SHELLS, TOO FEW HIGH-EXPLOSIVE SHELLS

Two types of shell were mainly used: shrapnel-type fragmentation shells and high-explosive shells. The former were adjusted to explode above the soil, throwing hundreds of spinning, glowing metallic projectiles into the air over a large area. These shells were very effective against soldiers advancing in the open field. They could be employed to destroy barbed-wire networks, tearing them to pieces. But they were practically useless against trenches dug into the ground, to say nothing of concrete-reinforced shelters. They nevertheless constituted the majority of shells fired by the British over the week-long preliminary bombardment. Destroying buried (and often concrete-reinforced) fortifications required high-explosive shells that could smash their targets in high-intensity detonations.

## Too many shells failed to explode

Too many of the shells fired that week simply failed to explode, plunging into the ground without causing particular damage. While the quantity of shells produced in Great Britain had begun to increase in early 1916, quality control remained a problem. Massively increasing the output of munitions had required that a wide variety of factories – including workshops not equipped for this type of manufacture – be converted to shell production. Many specialized munitions-factory workers had left for the front[56] and had been by replaced with inexperienced female workers. In 1915, a lack of shells limited the firepower of British artillery and, despite censorship, the subject had become a matter of public controversy in the press. An energetic figure – the future prime minister, Lloyd George – was thus appointed minister of munitions. Production volume finally increased in early 1916, but, in keeping with a commonplace bureaucratic phenomenon, at no point did anyone within the hierarchy take any pains to verify its quality. The result was that, in 1916, a large number of shells exploded in the guns' barrels, disintegrated in flight or, above all, failed to explode upon impact. It is not known what proportion of the shells fired in the course of the preliminary bombardment was defective but this doubtless concerned at least a third of all projectiles. From the end of the war and continuing for dozens of years afterwards, battlefield strollers could risk their lives by handling unexploded shells that they had disinterred or that had in one way or another risen once again to the surface. The Somme *département*'s mine-clearing service was thus guaranteed work for years to come.

## BARBED-WIRE NETWORKS LEFT INTACT

As we have seen, the use of shrapnel-type shells to destroy barbed-wire networks required great expertise on the part of artillerymen if they were to adjust the height of the explosion appropriately – a type of expertise sorely lacking among British artillerymen at this time. For the most part, the work of cutting the barbed wire was in various places carried out at ground level by sappers using large wire cutters. For the British, the result was disastrous: the attackers were channelled through a limited number of openings in the barbed-wire networks, allowing German machine-gunners to concentrate their fire without having to sweep the battlefield. On 1 July, the bodies piled up in front of these openings made in the German wire.

## INADEQUATE COUNTER-BATTERY FIRE

In the week preceding the attack, counter-battery fire relied on a mere 180 guns (out of 1,500) not tasked with directly bombarding enemy lines. It was the oldest and therefore least accurate of them that were used in the effort to destroy the batteries located behind the German trenches. In addition to the problems of inaccurate fire and defective ammunition, a large portion of the German artillery had not been located by the Allies. Given the French and British capacity for aerial surveillance, the Germans had for weeks chosen to camouflage a portion of their artillery, which waited for the attack to begin before opening fire. What's more, a large number of batteries had arrived on the Somme in the days preceding the attack and had thus still not been identified. Very disagreeably surprised by the intensity of German fire on 1 July, the British were unable to engage in effective counter-battery fire.

In addition to these reasons – all related to the operation of the artillery – there were a number of other factors, to do with the plan of attack itself.

## THE SEQUENCE AND TIMING OF THE ATTACK WERE POORLY CHOSEN

In order to hide the attackers' advance from the defenders' fire to the maximum extent, infantry attacks were as a rule launched at dawn. The choice to attack at 7.30 – and thus in the full sunlight of a July morning – required the British troops to advance in full view of German machine guns over a terrain that, after a week of bombardment, offered no relief or obstacles behind which to take cover, apart from shell holes.

In most cases, the five minutes separating the end of the British bombardment at 7.25 and the start of the infantry attack at 7.30 doubtless allowed the German defenders to leave their shelters and rush to their firing positions. In retrospect, British soldiers should have leaped over their parapets and crossed a portion of no man's land several minutes *before* the bombardment had ended rather than several minutes *after*. Indeed, that was the order here and there given by a few inspired battalion leaders: every time a local commander took the initiative to advance his men over no man's land before the bombardment's end and have them rush towards the enemy trench in order to reach it before the Germans left their shelters, casualties were much lower. On 1 July, the difference between a successful and failed attack was often a matter of minutes, even seconds.

## THE TROOPS WERE ADVISED TO ADVANCE IN A PERILOUS FORMATION

The British commander was aware that it would be a baptism of fire for most of the men attacking on that day. He was concerned to prevent this inexperienced army from scattering under fire, which would make it difficult for the officers to control their troops and render manoeuvre nearly impossible. It is for this reason that the men were instructed to advance as they did during exercises, marching in successive lines. At too many points along the front, however, the German machine-gun nests had not been destroyed. And when the terrain lacks all natural shelter, there is no worse formation in which to attack than to advance slowly in a line, the body upright. Too often, the German machine guns were able to almost mechanically mow down the wave of British foot soldiers as soon as the attack got under way. As we have seen, where battalion leaders gave the order to advance before 7.30 and move forward by leaps and starts, their units were generally decimated by the German artillery later in the day, between the first and second lines.

## INADEQUATE COMMUNICATIONS WITH THE ATTACKING TROOPS

Intended to allow the artillery's fire to track the attackers' advance and thereby supply them with adequate protection at all times, the notion of the rolling barrage was innovative. Yet it presupposed constant communication between attacking troops, artillerymen and the high command. On 1 July 1916, such communication was lacking or functioned poorly. The attackers thus very soon lost contact with the artillery that was supposed to cover their advance.

Entangled in the intact or only partially destroyed barbed-wire networks, in most cases the British soldiers watched as the impact of their artillery inexorably moved away in keeping with a fixed schedule.

The problem stemmed from what was at this stage the insufficient reliability of modern means of communication such as the telephone when employed by troops on the move and under fire. The artillery's fire thus had to advance mechanically without really being able to adapt to the actual progress of the infantry.

## THE INFORMATION THAT REACHED STAFF HEADQUARTERS WAS DELAYED AND FRAGMENTARY

In their respective chateaux, Haig and Rawlinson spent most of the day attempting to form an at once precise and comprehensive idea of the unfolding battle. With more than thirty distinct engagements under way over a twenty-kilometre front, staff headquarters was on the receiving end of a constant flow of information. The problem was that, in the absence of communications with the most forward positions, these reports were for the most part sent by observers who had remained in the rear.

Too often, this information was confused, incomplete and contradictory. For staff headquarters, it was very difficult to perceive the actual development of fighting in real time or even at a short delay. Uncertainty, confusion and the 'fog of war' extensively discussed by John Keegan[57] resulted in a lack of reliable information and gradually paralysed decision-making. It was thus with weary scepticism that, at midday, General Rawlinson greeted the news of the French army's (real) successes and the progress made by the British units adjoining them. With little confidence in his perception of the reality on the ground and still smarting from that morning's over-optimistic reports, Rawlinson failed to seize what was doubtless the only opportunity of the entire offensive to penetrate deeply enemy lines.

## EFFECTIVE AND WELL-CONCEIVED ENTRENCHMENTS

Many commentators have described the Battle of the Somme as 'modern siege warfare'. Yet less than two years earlier, the use of high-calibre German mortar fire to crush the forts of Liège had been interpreted as putting an end to the very possibility of siege warfare. Everything changed, however, when the single, massive, above-ground fortification was replaced by hundreds of concrete-reinforced shelters buried deep underground and distributed over the length of the front. The result was a new form of siege warfare that took place over an expanse of several dozen kilometres.

These shortcomings of the British plan were all compounded by the exceptional fighting spirit of the German troops, who it must be emphasized were every bit the equals of their French counterparts outside Verdun.

## DISCIPLINED GERMAN TROOPS WITH HIGH MORALE

It would be difficult to ignore the fact that, in addition to all of the other factors mentioned above, the fierce resistance of German troops – first under bombardment, then in the course of fighting – played an absolutely fundamental role in the British failure. The Germans had long been present on the Somme and had a perfect knowledge of the terrain. They were also fully convinced that, by holding this ground far from the Rhine at whatever cost, they were protecting their families and homeland from the horrors of war. A parallel might well be drawn with the behaviour of the French troops who confronted the German onslaught at Verdun in February 1916.

In this connection, the opening passage of German Second

Army commander General von Below's orders for 3 July 1916 deserves to be quoted:

> The outcome of the war depends on the Second Army being victorious on the Somme. Despite the current enemy superiority in artillery and infantry we have got to win this battle. The large areas of ground that we have lost in certain places will be attacked and wrested back from the enemy, just as soon as the reinforcements which are on the way arrive. For the time being, we must hold our current positions without fail and improve on them by means of minor counter-attacks. I forbid the voluntary relinquishing of positions. Every commander is responsible for making each man in the army aware about this determination to fight it out. The enemy must be made to pick his way forward over corpses.[58]

## AN OUTMODED HIGH COMMAND?

Finally, even with a century's hindsight, is it possible to judge the British high command dispassionately? Does the terse judgement ('Lions led by donkeys!') of an American journalist who witnessed a British assault against the Russian fortress of Sebastopol during the Crimean War remain relevant?

Even for today's historian, who is assumed to be dispassionate, it seems nearly impossible to issue a formal judgement as to the responsibility of British military and civilian leaders in what was unquestionably a bloody failure.

That elected politicians are absolutely pre-eminent over soldiers in determining the conduct of the war is today a fundamental axiom of the workings of Western democracies. At the beginning of the First World War, the principal responsibility for operations in both France and Britain unquestionably fell to soldiers – and, in particular, the commander-in-chief – once the conflict was under way. The latter decided nearly all questions as he pleased. The first duty of the minister of war, whether soldier or civilian, was to supply him with the human and material resources he required. In France, this only changed with Joffre's dismissal in December 1916 and above all following Georges Clemenceau's accession to power in 1917. Clemenceau had until then been a constant parliamentary and journalistic critic of the high command. His appointment to lead the government allowed him to begin applying his famous maxim: 'War is too important to be left to the generals.' In Great Britain, the War Cabinet kept what was doubtless a closer eye over military leaders than did its counterpart in France, as General French would learn at his expense in late 1915. But neither the minister of war, Lord Kitchener, nor the prime minister, Herbert Asquith, truly had the resources (in the case of Kitchener) or will (in that of Asquith) to weigh in decisively upon the decisions of the general staff. Most decisions were taken by the commander-in-chief of British forces on the French front, General Haig, even if, for reasons of temperament or respect, he chose not to systematically impose his views on subordinates such as Rawlinson, who was in charge of the Fourth Army. Throughout the Battle of the Somme, as a result, the nature of the objective that was to be pursued remained ill-defined: did it seek decisively to break through German defences or to gradually wear down the enemy's resources and reserves?

The war's military leaders were generally showered with praise during and immediately after the conflict. In the second half of the twentieth century, however, a highly critical revisionist view began to take hold. In popular culture, at least, this ultimately took the form of a grotesque (but sometimes amusing!) representation nicely illustrated, for example, by Richard Attenborough's film *Oh! What a Lovely War* (1969). According to this view, the war's military leaders, particularly the British ones, were idiots or psychopaths when they were not both.

In general, however, they were neither of these things. At the start of the conflict, by contrast, two major structural weaknesses hampered their ability to carry out their duties. These were men who had reached the summit of the chain of command and were thus nearly at the end of their careers. Nothing in their past experience – whether that of Haig in Sudan and South Africa, for example, or that of Joffre in Madagascar – had prepared them for their present task: to lead a largely industrial war at the head of a mass army. And, to be fair, no one among the military leaders of the various belligerents possessed this type of competence in 1914. Managing the articulation of modern firepower, wireless communications and a host of new weapons called for new skills – skills that were only gradually developed in the field by the leaders of the time and, above all, their younger subordinates, who often ended up replacing them.

It must be underscored, moreover, that the early twentieth century witnessed an unprecedented technological revolution in warfare as disruptive as the advent of the Internet has recently proven for the media.[59] Finally, this revolution was fuelled by constant feedback from four years of fighting: by 1918, automobile logistics, radio communications, new or modified weapons (such as tanks and aeroplanes) and heavy artillery had achieved a level of efficiency that still seemed very far off in 1916. The leaders of the time thus had to work with new but still imperfect and constantly changing tools, the basic use of which, moreover, had yet to be mastered. The development of the 'war of materiel' in any case made offensive operations extremely costly in terms of men at this time. In 1918, their successors would have the advantage of several years' newly acquired experience of the rapidly evolving techniques of combat.

# CHAPTER 14

## THE BATTLE OF THE SOMME FROM 2 JULY

The fighting resumed on the morning of 2 July. It was to continue for another four and a half months until mid-November 1916, when the arrival of the autumn rains, coupled with the exhaustion of men and materiel, prompted a (temporary) halt to operations. In the meantime, a series of local clashes lasting several days succeeded one another along various parts of the front. None of them were to prove decisive but all would be extremely bloody.

With the fighting of summer and autumn 1916, a large number of units from the British Dominions entered the fray: Australians, New Zealanders, South Africans, Canadians and so on. To this day, in fact, and in a way that is completely unsuspected in France, the names of particular villages and even particular hamlets and localities of the Somme such as Delville Wood and Mametz continue to resonate on the other side of the world, across the Atlantic and at the tip of Africa.

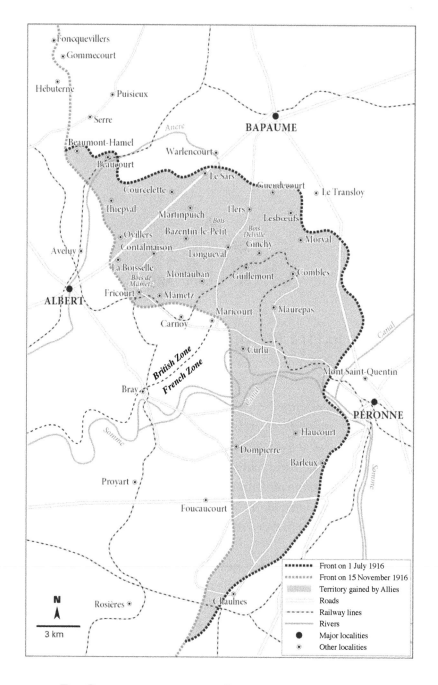

Front on 1 July 1916
Front on 15 November 1916
Territory gained by Allies
Roads
Railway lines
Rivers
Major localities
Other localities

THE SOMME FRONT BETWEEN GOMMECOURT AND PÉRONNE
ON 15 NOVEMBER 1916

As soon as the French and British realized that the lack of a decisive outcome on the afternoon of 1 July meant there would be no breakthrough, they began to clash over whether – and, above all, where – to resume the attack. Haig, who had begun to grasp the scale of casualties suffered by his two armies in comparison with their meagre gains, was tempted to play for time. He preferred to let the French pursue their operation and at the very least see how it developed north of the Somme before once again sending his troops into battle. Warned by Foch of Haig's intentions, Joffre rushed to the latter's headquarters at Beauquesne. As recounted by Maxime Weygand (Foch's chief of staff and future supreme commander in 1940), their exchange illustrates both Joffre's sometimes volcanic temper and his influence over his very refined British counterpart:

> General Joffre [...] asked Sir Douglas Haig to go back on his decision. The latter, very much in control of himself, declared this impossible. General Joffre took an increasingly severe tone to encourage him to carefully think things through since France had its eyes on him. His interlocutor, his face expressionless, did not answer. There was a moment of silence and then Joffre exploded in anger. Pounding his fist on the table hard enough to break it, he said: You will attack! With these words, he stood up and took leave of his host, who, pale and still polite, walked him to his car and along the way made an appointment with General Foch to reach an agreement with him regarding what was to be done about the attacks.[60]

The desire of the British to continue offensive operations on the Somme every so often needed to be shored up by the French leaders. Given the casualties of that summer, King George V, President Poincaré, Joffre and Haig even found it necessary to lunch together on 12 August. This meeting confirmed that the offensive would be pursued and thus went well from the French point of view.[61]

True to their word, the British thus continued to attack throughout the summer and autumn. These successive offensives had three characteristics in common. They no longer concerned the entire front of 1 July but rather more limited segments of several kilometres at a time. They drew upon huge numbers of fresh but often inexperienced troops recently arrived from faraway Dominions – Australians, New Zealanders, South Africans and Canadians. Finally, they gave rise, with mixed results, to a number of technical and tactical innovations in the use of artillery and aviation, and above all witnessed the first appearance of tanks on the battlefield.

Yet all of the operations on the Somme suffered from the same difficulties that condemned the 1 July offensive:

- A lack of clarity in regards to the objective to be pursued: to break through the enemy line or weaken it by means of the gradual and systematic attrition of its defences and reserves?
- The inefficiency and inadequate density of British long-range artillery.
- Chronic problems in coordinating the operations of French and British troops.
- Finally, exceptionally bad weather over the course of the summer and autumn of 1916, which put offensive operations at a disadvantage.

In chronological order, the main British attacks of that summer, henceforth reliant upon very large contingents of Dominion troops, were as follows:

## THE BATTLE OF BAZENTIN RIDGE

At dawn on 14 July, four British divisions outside Pozières, on the Albert–Bapaume axis, attacked along a five-kilometre front towards the villages of Bazentin-le-Petit, Bazentin-le-Grand and Longueval. At the tactical level, some lessons had already been drawn from the failures of 1 July. The attack was launched before dawn, at 3.25 in the morning. It was preceded by an extremely violent bombardment but one that only lasted five minutes, during which the first attack wave crawled as close as possible to the German positions. In fact, most of the day's objectives were achieved on schedule. Once again, the difficulty would be in exploiting this initial success.

## THE BATTLE OF DELVILLE WOOD

In order to secure the right flank of the British advance on Bazentin and Longueval, it was necessary to seize a wooded prominence known as Delville Hill. This fighting marked the first engagement of the South African Brigade (which also included a Rhodesian regiment) on the Western Front. After heavy fighting, the South Africans succeeded in taking the wood. It was nevertheless retaken by the Germans, who were only to be permanently driven out on 3 September.

In five days, from 15 July to 20 July, the brigade lost more than 2,500 men killed and wounded.

## The Battle of Fromelles

Further to the west, Haig sent the soldiers of the 5th Australian Division to attack in the sector of Fromelles on 19 July. It was to be their baptism of fire on the Western Front. They collided with the first reinforcements that Falkenhayn had withdrawn from the Verdun front and dispatched to the Somme. The presence of these unanticipated reinforcements threw the battle in the Germans' favour. In Australian memory, the extremely violent fighting that followed came to represent the darkest twenty-four hours of the country's history. Over the course of the day, the British lost 7,000 killed and wounded, including more than 5,500 Australians.

## The Battle of Pozières Hill

Conducted by the 1st Australian Division, the Battle of Pozières Hill on 23 July marked a new attempt to take control of the village of Pozières. It immediately triggered a violent German counter-attack, which lasted until 7 August. Over the course of the same month, military operations on both sides were seriously slowed by frequent bad weather, which further complicated the attackers' job. In September, hostilities resumed at an intense pace with a violent German counter-attack on 3 September against the village of Guillemont, which had been taken on 1 July.

## The Battle of Ginchy

The exceptionally rainy month of August 1916 had slowed offensive operations. They vigorously resumed in early September, allowing the Irish 16th Division (the Catholic and nationalist counterpart of the 36th Ulster Division, which had taken the Schwaben Redoubt on 1 July) to win renown in its turn. The capture of the village of Ginchy on 9 September, combined with the success of a massive French attack on the 12th, strained the German defenders and allowed the Allies to position themselves for a major new attack in mid-September: the Battle of Flers–Courcelette.

## THE BATTLE OF FLERS–COURCELETTE

This British offensive in the direction of Morval and Gueudecourt was combined with a French attack towards Frégicourt and Rancourt. The fighting was marked by both human and technological novelty. For one thing, it marked the first appearance of Canadian and New Zealander troops in the Battle of the Somme. But, above all, it witnessed the first battlefield appearance of British tanks. Apart from the initial surprise they caused, their use was at this stage a failure. The machines of September 1916 were still too heavy and too easily damaged, as well as being under-motored and under-gunned.

## THE FIGHTING OF AUTUMN 1916

Given the repeated attacks that took place on the Somme front between early July and mid-November 1916, one may legitimately wonder whether the British high command had successfully advanced on the 'learning curve' in managing its offensives. For this period, that does not seem to have been the case.[62] Despite tactical and technical improvements and the arrival of fresh troops into the fray, the Allies were unable to push back the German lines significantly, much less break through them. Now heavily reinforced by troops and materiel transferred from the Verdun front, the German defence continued to hold. Yet German casualties accumulated. September was accompanied by the highest German casualties of the battle. German planners constantly worried about the overall numerical inferiority of their army relative to the Allied army total. They now began to worry about what was in the process of becoming a battle of attrition. In this type of confrontation, the enemy is defeated not by a decisive victory, but by the exhaustion of his human and material resources. Given the effective Allied blockade and the human resources available to the French and British empires, it was this that German strategists feared more than anything else. Within the German general staff, a debate thus developed regarding the prospect of 'shortening the lines' by withdrawing to new fortified positions to the rear rather than immediately and systematically counter-attacking, as had been the army's practice since autumn 1914.

A rainy August was followed by yet worse weather in the autumn. It was thus in difficult climatic and material conditions that the British and French launched their offensives against Le Transloy,[63] Thiepval and the valley of the Ancre (a small tributary of the Somme) in October and November. These attacks were to be the last of the battle, which is considered to have ended on 18 November, the 141st day of the offensive that began on 1 July. However, it was in no way the last time fighting was to occur in these places over the course of the First World War.

Bad weather, now intensified by freezing cold (and combined with the troops' exhaustion), convinced the Allied general staffs to suspend operations. This period of relative calm was to last less than two months. Allied attacks resumed in mid-January 1917 and continued until mid-February. The Germans then undertook a thirty-kilometre planned withdrawal towards what had been dubbed the 'Hindenburg Line', a line of fortified positions dug over the preceding months.

The zone running from Bapaume to Péronne and passing through Albert was thus spared fighting for a time. This respite was to be short-lived, however: before the end of the conflict, the armies would twice more cross over the Somme front – first in one direction and then the other

– bringing devastation in their wake. First came the last-chance German offensive of spring 1918 that preceded the massive influx of American troops. In just a few days, all of the terrain won from the Germans over the course of the ten preceding months was lost – and then some. But the German operation ran out of steam and their advance was stopped by Allied troops after bitter fighting. In Australian memory, in particular, the 25 April fighting at Villers-Bretonneux is seen as a great victory.

It would be from the Somme front, finally, that a decisive Allied counter-offensive was to be launched against the German army. On 8 August, what the German general Erich Ludendorff called 'the black day of the German army' took place in the vicinity of Moreuil. On that day, an Allied attack succeeded in advancing more than ten kilometres in a single day while taking a large number of prisoners and forcing the German army into a retreat that would continue almost without interruption until 11 November. Throughout the conflict, the Somme was thus a veritable 'corridor of death' on the Western Front.

# CHAPTER 15

## THE CONSEQUENCES OF THE BATTLE OF THE SOMME

### THE HUMAN CONSEQUENCES

It is important to underline once again the uncertainty that hangs over battlefield casualty figures for the First World War, particularly in what concerns the exact number of dead. It is generally held that the Battle of the Somme began with the start of the British preliminary bombardment on 25 June 1916, and continued until the failure of the final offensive on 15 November. Over the course of this five-month period, there were roughly 420,000 casualties (killed, wounded and missing) among the soldiers of Great Britain and its Dominions.[64] On top of this total were more than 200,000 French and at least 400,000 German casualties.

Whatever uncertainty may surround these figures, the Battle of the Somme was clearly the bloodiest confrontation to take place on the Western Front over the course of the First World

War. In Great Britain, the immediate impact of these casualties was of course devastating. In part, this was due to their scale: for example, nearly twice as many British soldiers were casualties of the Battle of the Somme as had disembarked at the Channel ports with the BEF two years earlier. This was compounded by the very structure of the 'New Army', which was made up of pals battalions often recruited along geographical lines. When a regiment was dissolved under fire, this ensured that the impact was immense in the localities and regions from which the vast majority of its soldiers had been drawn. In the same way, the heavy losses sustained by the young nations of the British Dominions – hitherto spared the bloody military episodes that had punctuated the history of European nations – were to mark their as yet inchoate collective memories. The names of Beaumont-Hamel, Delville, La Boisselle and Pozières are virtually unknown in France today yet continue to resonate deeply from Cape Town to Melbourne, from St John's in Newfoundland to Auckland in New Zealand.

As was generally the case over the course of the conflict, the Germans' choice of a defensive posture meant that they suffered only a fraction (though still around 70 per cent) of the attackers' casualties. In absolute terms, however, the number of soldiers killed in action was still very high. What's more, they consisted of experienced, battle-hardened soldiers who would be sorely missed over the course of the next two years. As a result of the high casualties sustained on the Somme, the German ministry of war decided to implement its planned call-up of 400,000 men ahead of schedule.[65] Aware of the overall numerical inferiority of Germany and Austria-Hungary in comparison with the Entente nations, the German general staff was very eager to avoid simultaneously sustaining large-scale casualties at two separate points on the Western Front. This was one of the factors in its decision to begin scaling back operations on the Verdun front in mid-July. The scale of casualties led the German general staff to launch a propaganda campaign targeting the German civilian population. Its theme: 'The German soldiers of the Somme are heroes. Their sacrifice has saved German territory from the devastations of this terrible war.' The 'Song of the 180th', which celebrates the actions of that Swabian regiment in the fighting on the Somme in 1916, thus proclaims:

> The remains of the walls of Thiepval tremble
> At the bottom of holes and trenches;
> The Swabian listens carefully:
> It's Württemberger soil,
> Said General von Soden,
> He who wants it has to pay the price.[66]

As a theme, what's more, the defence of national soil in foreign territory would be abundantly taken up following the country's defeat in 1918. During the Weimar Republic, German nationalists drew upon it to justify the fact that the war had been allowed to continue for more than four years. The Nazis then used it to explain the Third Reich's policy of aggression. Alongside its racial and economic components, the Hitlerian policy of *Lebensraum* (living space) also sought to create a strategic buffer around German-speaking populations.

In France, by contrast, the battle had less of an impact on public life. Although relatively few in the battle's first days, French casualties considerably increased over the course of the late summer and early autumn. They nevertheless remained below the figures that had been accepted as the price of defending Verdun (where 163,000 French troops were killed in 1916). Here as elsewhere, the public's attention was monopolized by the latter front, where the stand taken by the French army and its thoroughly legitimate defensive position suffered no competition from its British ally.

## THE STRATEGIC CONSEQUENCES

As we have seen, the breakthrough never took place. From the point of view of territorial gains, the results were negligible after five months of fighting. Over a twelve-kilometre front, the Allies succeeded in taking a swath of territory between five and nine kilometres deep – that is, not even as much as was envisaged in the most limited objectives of the offensive's first day. In what was a cruel irony, most of that hard-fought territory would be conquered without resistance in early 1917 after the Germans retreated to the 'Hindenburg Line'.

It is true that, as the French and British generals hoped, the Germans gradually withdrew troops and artillery pieces from the Verdun front from mid-July and over the course of the summer, transferring them to the Somme and elsewhere. But it may legitimately be wondered whether these withdrawals would not have occurred in any case, with Falkenhayn finally accepting that his campaign on the Meuse had failed and proving eager to redeploy his forces outside France and, in particular, to the Eastern Front.

With Hindenburg as supreme commander, in September 1916 Falkenhayn was replaced by Ludendorff, quartermaster general of the German army. He in this way paid for the German failure at Verdun. Following his appointment, Ludendorff travelled to the Western Front, his first visit there since leaving for the Eastern Front in late August 1914. On the basis of his observation of the situation, in particular on the Somme, he became convinced that the war in the west had entered a new phase in which the generals' skill and the men's value hardly mattered any more. It had become a war of industrial attrition, a war of materiel.[67]

As the German army's de facto leader, Ludendorff's

conclusions profoundly transformed the manner in which the Germans conducted the war. First came the decision to militarize fully the German economy. In October 1916, Hindenburg and Ludendorff launched an ambitious programme to double the production of military materiel and supplies in the space of virtually one year. To do so, the German state more directly intervened in the allocation of the economy's material, financial and human resources. The objective was to devote nearly all available resources to increasing incessantly the production of weapons and munitions to the detriment of civilian goods. It was from this time, in fact, that restrictions and hardship began to affect severely the civilian population. This growing hardship, in its turn, began to affect the morale of German troops, who took note of it in the course of their (relatively infrequent) period of home leave.

In what was a logical extension of the German conversion to industrial war, the new German general staff then persuaded the government to launch unrestricted submarine warfare so as to hamper the Allied industrial effort to the maximum extent. This strategic decision, which authorized the merchant marine vessels of neutral countries to be torpedoed, was in its turn among the factors that induced the United States to enter the war in 1917. The contrast is thus immense between the minute territorial outcomes of the Battle of the Somme and its strategic consequences.

## POLITICAL CONSEQUENCES

In Great Britain, the Asquith government did not long survive the operations on the Somme. Asquith was at the head of a national-unity government that was never formally removed from office. His departure was the result of discussions between the various parties, including his own Liberal Party. Above all, his ouster – because that is what it was – reflected the erosion of his personal leadership within the political class. In addition to the bloody failure on the Somme, he was among other things criticized for his personal style, in particular his nearly religious habit of passing all of his evenings in games of bridge. With increasing frequency, his penchant for alcohol prevented him from participating in late-afternoon and evening debates in the House of Commons. Nor, it should be noted, was his dependence improved by the death of his adored eldest son, Raymond, on the Somme in September 1916.[68] The degree to which Great Britain was at the time characterized by marked class distinctions also bears repeating. It must be admitted that the British ruling class was not miserly in sacrificing its male children, immense numbers of whom enlisted as subaltern officers, a group with higher casualties than any other throughout the conflict.[69]

By contrast, the foremost British military leaders in France – Haig, of course, but also Rawlinson, the commander of the Fourth Army – kept their posts. Despite an unfathomable number of casualties, the failure to break through enemy lines and meagre territorial gains, it would take time before the Somme offensive came to be seen as an unmitigated disaster.[70]


In France, a last-ditch ministerial reshuffle in late December allowed prime minister Aristide Briand to survive 1916.

As minister of war, he appointed General Hubert Lyautey. Lyautey was a personal enemy of Joffre, who had gradually been abandoned by most of his supporters in parliament. With the battles of Verdun and the Somme, the year had been particularly bloody and voters increasingly made their exhaustion and suffering known to politicians. Many of them now sought to travel to the front or as close as possible to the trenches in order to investigate personally the conduct of military operations. This did not suit Joffre at all, who was not keen to 'have politicians underfoot'. Moreover, he feared that the military leaders at Verdun – in particular, Pétain and Nivelle – would play up their roles at the expense of his own. With the help of his staff, in short, he threw as many roadblocks as possible in the way of parliamentary missions before Briand finally concluded that he had more to gain than to lose from Joffre's departure. On 26 December 1916, it was done: Joffre was promoted to the rank of Marshal of France. Completely sidelined, he was not consulted on the choice of his successor, General Nivelle. In addition to being a specialist in artillery operations, Nivelle had the advantage of an English mother and a fluent command of that language. From the point of view of British involvement, that was now an important consideration in leading French armies...

In Germany, Falkenhayn was replaced in late August by the team of Hindenburg and Ludendorff (whose title, 'quartermaster general', nicely reflects the importance assigned the war of materiel and its influence on the organization of the German economy). Yet his record on the Somme was not dishonourable: like the French soldiers at Verdun, the German soldiers under Falkenhayn's command held their positions in particularly difficult circumstances. But he paid for the failure at Verdun and, above all, the rising casualties of the German army over the course of 1916.

## Military consequences

### Technological developments

In 1916, the conflict evolved into a modern form of siege warfare after the massive, blind and brutal use of artillery had proven ineffective in clearing a path. Henceforth, the French and British high commands would turn to technological innovation to escape from the tactical and strategic rut in which they had become stuck. Working independently of one another, soldiers with a technical and entrepreneurial bent – Ernest Swinton in Great Britain, Jean Baptiste Eugène Estienne in France – developed the idea of mobile, armoured artillery capable of accompanying the infantry over devastated battlefields by virtue of tracked movement.

It is this that explains the appearance of the Mark I, Britain's first tank, on the battlefield outside Flers on 15 September 1916. Apart from its surprise effect, its initial impact was rather limited. The tanks' tactical failure on the Somme convinced German military leaders that it was not fundamentally necessary to develop this weapon. The German army was in the process of developing a form of tactical assault based on the speed and initiative of small, specialized assault groups. These new tactics were implemented in 1917 but were above all to play a prominent role in the course of the Germans' last offensive in spring 1918. Tanks such as those that were manoeuvred on the Somme would have slowed these groups down and, in any case, the Germans quickly learned how to use artillery fire efficiently to neutralize these fragile mastodons. Lastly, it was believed that there were more important priorities for German steel production.

Alongside aerial duels, the aviation of 1914 now took on the reconnaissance role traditionally played by the cavalry: the observation of enemy movements.[71] As these machines' technical capacities improved, their role was extended to new missions such as fighting and bombardment. The Battle of the Somme would witness other advances, including the use of aerial radio communications to adjust artillery fire. It was on the Somme, finally, that the aeroplanes first conducted strafing runs against enemy trenches in support of infantry attack. The aeroplane in this way also became a ground attack weapon.

## The fighting on the Somme rapidly led to tactical developments on both sides

Never again would the British carry out a week-long bombardment followed by an advance of infantry marching in line. Henceforth, bombardments would be intense but short and coupled with a more fluid infantry advance. The result was a much greater number of successful attacks against the German front lines. The continued absence of effective systems of communication and coordination, by contrast, continued to hamper efforts to exploit these initial successes, with the Germans each time succeeding in plugging gaps in their lines.

The Germans, for their part, relaxed their tactical defence procedures. When coming under intense fire, the number of front-line troops was often reduced, with most troops drawing back a short distance. The objective of this in-depth defence was to limit casualties and entrust the task of counter-attacking to men who had not been subjected to quite so much strain.

## The moral consequences

Despite the failure of the British offensive, the Battle of the Somme was to leave its greatest mark on the German high command and German combatants. Until that point, Germany's military and civilian leadership had been nearly convinced that they would win the war. While it is true that the Schlieffen Plan's lightning offensive had failed, the defensive posture that the Germans had adopted on the Western Front since October 1914 allowed the Allied offensives of 1915 to be repelled, with enormous casualties for the attackers. Germany remained persuaded that Allied public opinion, particularly in France, would tire of this slaughter and push its leaders to sue for a negotiated peace. The peace terms leaked by the Germans in response to the overtures of neutral countries in late 1915 reflected their confident belief that they could win on the Western Front as well as against Russia. This perception gradually changed in 1916 with the battles of Verdun and the Somme: what began to emerge was a war of attrition and exhaustion. Increasingly, German leaders worried that they were incapable of winning the war. They lacked the demographic resources, especially since the growing weakness of their Austrian ally was forcing them constantly to divert their already limited human resources to compensate for its failures. Nor did they have the necessary material resources. Unlike French industry, it is true, German industry did not suffer amputation or destruction. Increasingly, however, the maritime blockade was taking its toll. The German economy of 1914 was very open to the external world and the conflict pitted it against long-standing customers and suppliers. The blockade had, moreover, inflicted very severe blows and, increasingly, this had repercussions on the supplies available to the population – a population, what's more, that was aware of the war's rapidly rising casualties, even if the German army was holding its positions.

The Battle of the Somme's effect on civilians varied from one country to the next.

It was in the British world, of course, that the battle's human losses were most keenly felt. In 1914 and 1915, British casualties had been relatively limited, both numerically and in terms of the social strata that were affected, and this for a simple reason: a relatively small number of troops had been sent into battle. Those killed were either long-serving professional soldiers or drawn from territorial units. As soon as the soldiers of Kitchener's Army began to swell British ranks in France and these units were gradually sent into battle over the course of 1916, the number of killed and wounded very rapidly increased. These new casualties affected entire swaths of the population and, in particular, the urban middle classes, which had not traditionally supplied recruits to Britain's professional army but were over-represented in that of Kitchener. From the summer of 1916, all of British society was deeply affected.

The British offensive of 1 July 1916 was marked by an entirely unprecedented and novel event: the preparation and first moments of the offensive were filmed on location and in real time.[72] Produced between mid-June and mid-July 1916, the film was quite a technical feat given the extremely difficult conditions on the ground and the equipment of the time (the tripod-mounted, hand-cranked cameras tended to expose their operators, making the work very dangerous). Above all, the cameramen had been allowed to film preparations for the attack freely, even following the troops as they assembled in the departure trenches, and, at 7.20 in the morning on 1 July, were able to capture the explosion of the Hawthorn Ridge mine outside Beaumont-Hamel. By contrast, several scenes meant to depict the attack itself were in reality re-enactments produced in mid-July. A short scene of roughly ten seconds nevertheless seems actually to provide absolutely gripping, authentic images of an initial British assault wave being mowed down by German machine-gun fire. The film-makers captured the immediate consequences of the attack, showing the corpses of British and German soldiers alike. And of course there were images of German prisoners, some able-bodied, others wounded. In a completely unheard-of move, however, the film also shows British wounded, many of whom would have been perfectly recognizable to their loved ones and were clearly in great pain. The film was rapidly edited between late July and early August with significant involvement on the part of the British military authorities. Silent and in black and white, the film lasts seventy-seven minutes and is divided into roughly fifty sequences, each preceded by an explanatory insert. On 10 August, the film premiered before an audience of journalists and military leaders. It was an unprecedented, immediate and stunning success in Great Britain. In six weeks, it had been seen by more than 20 million people. For the first time, the British were allowed a visual representation of the reality of the fighting in which their sons, brothers and fathers were participating in France, including its cruellest and most gruesome aspects. In addition to being a huge popular success, the film was generally very well received in political circles – although it was criticized, particularly by the clergy, for its depiction of corpses and the suffering of British wounded.

In September, the film was also shown to British troops in France, in particular those who had participated in the 1 July attack. Rapidly exported abroad, it had been shown in eighteen countries by the end of the war.

Its success did not go unnoticed by the German high command, which thus decided to make its own film, simply titled *With Our Heroes on the Somme*.[73] The German film, which mainly consists of re-enacted combat scenes filmed behind the lines after the event, lacks its British counterpart's apparent authenticity. Nor did it enjoy the same success, despite support from the authorities.

## THE CONSEQUENCES FOR MEMORY

In the years immediately following the conflict, the traces left in memory by the battle varied widely from one nation to the next. In particular, the official histories assembled by general staffs in the post-war years were as eloquent in terms of what they passed over as in what they said. The official, 107-volume French chronicle, *Les Armées françaises dans la Grande Guerre*, devotes merely five pages to the events of

1 July 1916, only one paragraph of which discusses the British attack... The handful of lines devoted to the bloodiest day in their ally's history by the French military chroniclers can be quoted in full:

> On the English front, the Fourth Army's progress was checked around noon. By means of energetic counter-attacks, the enemy nearly everywhere drove back the 8th, 10th and 3rd British corps – that is, the left wing and centre – to their starting positions, and at the end of the day Rawlinson's army only really held the hilltop between La Boisselle and Fricourt and the villages of Mametz and Montauban.[74]

That's it.

The proportion was roughly the same in the case of the British. The *British Official History*, published in 109 volumes between 1915 and 1949, devotes six chapters to this single day but only one page to the French offensive. On both sides, these historical chronicles were written and edited in the 1920s by high-ranking officers who had been present for the fighting at the time of the battle. Their selective 'memory' of the events casts light on the difficulty experienced by French and British generals in effectively collaborating on the Somme in July 1916.

Among the British, the first years following the Armistice were above all marked by celebrations of the quiet and unfortunate heroism of the tens of thousands of young men who, on the morning of 1 July 1916, bravely advanced to their appalling fate. Little by little, however, the action – or inaction – of the British military leaders came to be called into question.

Today, the battlefields of the Somme are sites of memory faithfully visited by the British. In addition to the many military cemeteries, remarkably well maintained by the Commonwealth War Graves Commission, the full length of the front is dotted with an impressive number of monuments. These sites are no longer visited by the war's veterans, who have been replaced by a mainly anglophone public of all ages (a significant proportion of whom are schoolchildren representing the fourth and fifth generations...).

To single out just some of the more notable sites:

- The Beaumont-Hamel Newfoundland Memorial
- The Canadian memorial at Courcelette
- The Franco-British memorial at Thiepval
- The Delville Wood South African National Memorial
- The New Zealand National Memorial at Longueval
- The 38th Welsh Division memorial at Mametz Wood.

By way of comparison, it is worth noting once again that on 22 August 1914 – the bloodiest day in French history – nearly 28,000 French soldiers were killed. A century later, on 22 August 2014, no official commemoration took place. By contrast, the British authorities expected so many people to attend the 1 July 2016 commemoration held for the 20,000 men who died on the Somme a century earlier that they set up an online lottery to distribute tickets.

## FRANCE AND BRITAIN IN THE WAR, FROM 1914 TO TODAY

The Battle of the Somme and the bloody paroxysm of its first day are central to the manner in which the British conceive of their relationship to Europe and, in particular, France. To say that Great Britain's place in Western Europe has always represented a difficult question for British and Europeans alike would be an understatement. The former have always swung between accepting – nay, desiring and demanding – membership in Europe's various political, economic, monetary and military incarnations and the temptation of insularity, of the 'open sea' and a 'privileged' Atlantic partnership with the United States. It has frequently seemed tempting to withdraw into oneself (and one's empire). Less familiar are the moments when the opposite extreme has reigned.

It is worth recalling here that, on 16 June 1940, with the Battle of France decisively turning to the Germans' advantage, General de Gaulle in London contacted the French premier, Paul Reynaud, then in Bordeaux: there, the latter was about to meet with his last cabinet to discuss a possible armistice with Germany. Through the intermediary of de Gaulle, Churchill, who had recently been appointed as prime minister, and his foreign secretary, Lord Halifax, suggested that the fight be continued by fully uniting the two nations of France and Great Britain. This historically extraordinary and unprecedented offer was immediately rejected by Raynaud's cabinet, which resigned that very evening to make room for Pétain.

The debate over the United Kingdom's place in Europe continues to this day and was put to a referendum in 2016. Most recently, the flow of refugees into Western Europe and the determination of some of them to enter Great Britain by way of France have given rise to what may seem a novel controversy: can the United Kingdom legitimately regard its border as passing through Calais? The historian of the First World War will content himself here with noting that, far from being novel, the question had already arisen in August 1914. Many in Britain argued – a perfectly reasonable position – that the country's true borders were located wherever the squadrons of the Royal Navy were stationed. With unanimous support from its Parliament and population, the British government ultimately decided that its border really did pass through Calais and the coast of Belgium. The potential invasion of the town by a hostile power such as Germany therefore represented a *casus belli* and justified the country's entry into the war, with all the consequences that that entailed.

Among them was the death of more than 750,000 citizens of the United Kingdom. When the Dominions and the rest of the empire are included, that figure reaches 950,000. The great majority of these soldiers were killed while fighting in France, including nearly 200,000 in the course of the 140 days of the Battle of the Somme. Of these, more than 20,000 died on 1 July 1916.

# CHAPTER 16

## RETURN TO BEAUMONT-HAMEL:
## A PATH OF MEMORY

The memorial to the soldiers of the Newfoundland Regiment is located in Beaumont-Hamel on the very site of the 1 July 1916 battlefield.

After the war, in 1922, the Newfoundland government purchased thirty-four hectares of land from more than 250 French owners, financing the operation by way of public subscription.

It was decided to keep the battlefield as it was and so partly maintain trenches and shelters. A commemorative monument was also built. It consists of a giant caribou that stands atop a small mound on a hill located at the level of the second line of British trenches. From here, it is possible to contemplate almost the entire battlefield, for the hill descends, gently sloping towards the little ravine 400 metres on where the German soldiers of the 119th Reserve Infantry Regiment had dug their deep and solid shelters. Since it ends in a fork, the

British named this area 'Ravine Y'. The slope of the hill is a bit more pronounced in the centre, giving it a bowl-like shape.

Arriving at the site, the visitor enters at the level of the first approach trenches, where the Newfoundland soldiers waited in the dark of night. A few hundred metres ahead of them, the men of the first two assault waves were massed in the first- and second-line trenches.

Today's visitor may in fact walk towards the first two lines: it is around 400 steps to the second line of trenches and 300 more steps to the front-line positions, the departure trenches. Done briskly but without running, it is a trip that takes under ten minutes. Under heavy artillery bombardment and entangled in their own barbed-wire networks, however, the Newfoundlander soldiers took more than half an hour to reach their destination on 1 July 1916, and immediately lost more than half of their strength. Having reached this point, the survivors toppled down the slope: alongside the bombardment, they were now in full view of the Germany machine guns, their silhouettes standing out distinctly on the horizon. Another 150 metres farther on, a little copse – one of which survives to this day, the aptly named 'Danger Tree' – marks the point where the largest number of corpses was found on this part of the battlefield. It was at this point that the still impenetrable German barbed-wire networks began. The contemporary visitor, for his part, can continue walking – only a few hundred steps remain to reach the German lines. There is no access to the German trenches as their dense array of half-collapsed underground shelters has destabilized the ground. The visitor may nevertheless enter the little cemetery of Ravine Y, which is located immediately front and centre of the German positions. There, he passes before 100 immaculate white stelae. Most bear names but some are simply inscribed with the words 'A soldier of the Great War'. Turning around, by contrast, he realizes that, from where he now stands, he has an unobstructed view of every centimetre of the terrain all the way up to the semicircular slope down which the attackers struggled to descend on 1 July.

From this point of view, it would seem impossible for a body of soldiers to advance without being exterminated by the defenders' fire. And, indeed, at no point in the Battle of the Somme did anyone succeed in doing so. The Scottish soldiers who finally took the German trenches four months later did so by applying siege-warfare techniques that had been codified by Vauban in the late eighteenth century. For weeks on end, they dug perpendicular trenches to allow them to advance towards the German lines. They then gradually linked these to one another in order to form new, ever more advanced trench lines. When they were finally close enough to the German lines, they took them in a last (bloody) assault.

At the foot of the caribou, a bronze plaque lists the names of the 814 Newfoundlander soldiers and sailors whose bodies, pulverized by shells, buried in mud or lying at the bottom of the sea, were never recovered. The monument was inaugurated in 1925 by Field Marshal Haig.

The site also includes three small cemeteries: that of Hawthorn Ridge, where an enormous mine was set off by the British; a cemetery dedicated to the 51st Scottish Highlanders Division; and the cemetery of Ravine Y. Within the last of these, the Newfoundlander soldiers who fell on 1 July 1916 lie side by side with the Gordon Highlanders, the Scottish soldiers who, on one of the last days of the Battle of the Somme, finally conquered the first German trench line.

On the first day of the offensive, this German trench had been the objective of the first assault wave. It was to have fallen within the first half-hour of fighting. In the event, it would take British soldiers four and a half months to cross the 400 metres separating them from the German positions.

While Scottish troops thus finally took the German positions, the soldiers of Newfoundland did not long remain at rest. After a few weeks in Flanders, during which the survivors mainly used their time to write to their families and those of their fallen comrades, the regiment once again set off for the Somme. In October 1916, it saw fighting outside Gueudecourt and, in 1917, participated in the battles of Arras and Cambrai, once again sustaining heavy casualties. Following the latter battle, King George V bestowed the epithet 'Royal' upon the regiment, which was henceforth to be known as the 'Royal Newfoundland'. It was the only time in the course of hostilities that such a title was awarded. The regiment again saw intense fighting in 1918, first to halt the Germans' spring offensive and then, from late summer onwards, in the course of the final Allied counter-offensive.

At the end of the conflict, the Royal Newfoundland had lost more than 1,300 men out of a total of 5,000 sent into battle. Several hundred other Newfoundlanders lost their lives while serving in the Royal Navy, the merchant marine or the Canadian army. The post-war period was difficult for those who returned to Newfoundland. The war had been difficult to finance. While it lasted, however, the economy had been buoyed by the reduced production of European fisheries, which drove up the price of cod, the country's economic mainspring. Once the war was over, competition from European fishermen resumed at the same time as the budgetary burden of various pensions (disability, widowhood, veterans, and so on) was putting a heavy strain on the country's finances. With the onset of the crisis of the 1930s, and despite the introduction (for the first time) of income tax and a reduction in veterans' pensions,[75] the government gradually found itself in a position of quasi-bankruptcy. Under the weight of its debt, it thus had to place itself under the economic protection of the United Kingdom, which appointed a commission to fiscally administer the country. The Second World War years provided a temporary respite for Newfoundland's economy and budget thanks to the income from ports rented to the Americans for the purpose of installing the naval and air bases needed to protect maritime traffic in the North Atlantic. At the end of the Second World War, however, Newfoundland's government, parliament and population ultimately concluded that the country no longer possessed the resources required for an independent existence. While some favoured joining the United States, in 1948 a narrow majority voted in favour of joining the Canadian Confederation, of which Newfoundland and Labrador would henceforth be a province.

It is thus clear that the independence of Newfoundland – a fragile society – did not survive the immense human and economic effort entailed by its (enthusiastic) decision to participate in the First World War and allow so many young volunteers to leave for it. With a population roughly equivalent to that of a mid-sized French city such as Dijon, the financial effort that this represented and, above all, the direct and indirect consequences of the war's casualties were more than the country could bear while maintaining its independence.


Before leaving the memorial, the visitor passes before a discreet stela bearing the following verses:

> Tread softly here! Go reverently and slow!
> Yea, let your soul go down upon its knees,
> And with bowed head and heart abased strive hard
> To grasp the future gain in this sore loss!
> For not one foot of this dank sod but drank
> Its surfeit of the blood of gallant men.
> Who, for their faith, their hope – for Life and Liberty,
> Here made the sacrifice – here gave their lives.
> And gave right willingly – for you and me.[76]

# BIBLIOGRAPHY

Audoin-Rouzeau, Stéphane, *Quelle histoire* (Paris: Gallimard, 2013).

— — — and Annette Becker, *14–18, retrouver la guerre* (Paris: Gallimard, 2000).

— — — and Jean-Jacques Becker, eds, *Encyclopédie de la Grande Guerre* (Paris: Bayard, 2004).

Axelrod, Alan, *The Battle of the Somme* (Guilford, CT: Lyons Press, 2016).

Barton, Peter, *The Somme* (London: Constable, 2006).

Bull, Stephen, *Trench: A History of Warfare on the Western Front* (Oxford: Osprey, 2010).

Cave, Nigel, *Beaumont Hamel* (London: Leo Cooper, 2010).

Corrigan, Gordon, *Mud, Blood and Poppycock* (London: Cassell, 2004).

Cosson, Olivier, *Préparer la Grande Guerre: l'armée française et la guerre russo-japonaise (1899–1914)* (Paris: Les Indes Savantes, 2013).

de Courcy, Anne, *Margot at War* (London: Weidenfeld & Nicolson, 2014).

Griffiths, William R., *The Great War* (1986; New York: Square One, 2003).

Hart, Peter, *The Great War: A Combat History of the First World War* (Oxford: Oxford University Press, 2013)

Horne, John, ed., *A Companion to World War I* (Oxford: Blackwell, 2010).

Jünger, Ernst, *Storm of Steel*, trans. Michael Hofmann (London: Penguin, 2003).

Keegan, John, *The Face of Battle* (London: Penguin, 1978).

Kendall, Paul, *Somme 1916: Success and Failure on the First Day of the Battle of the Somme* (Barnsley: Frontline, 2015).

Le Naour, Jean-Yves, *1916: l'enfer* (Paris: Perrin, 2014).

MacDonald, Lyn, *Somme* (London: Penguin, 2013).

Mace, Martin, and John Grehan, *Slaughter on the Somme: 1 July 1916: The Complete War Diaries of the British Army's Worst Day* (Barnsley: Pen & Sword, 2013).

Meyer, Jacques, *Ce qu'on voit d'une offensive* (Paris: Éditions des Malassis, 2014).

Middlebrook, Martin, *The First Day on the Somme: 1 July 1916* (1971; London: Penguin, 2006).

Miquel, Pierre, *Les oubliés de la Somme* (Paris: Tallandier, 2013).

Philpott, William, *Bloody Victory* (London: Little, Brown, 2009).

Poincaré, Raymond, *Mémoires*, vol. vi (Paris: Plon, 1930).

Prior, Robin, and Trevor Wilson, *The Somme* (New Haven, CT: Yale University Press, 2006).

Rawson, Andrew, *The Somme Campaign* (Barnsley: Pen & Sword, 2014).

Regan, Geoffrey, *Great Military Blunders* (London: Macmillan, 2000).

Robertson, Andrew, *Somme 1916* (Stroud: History Press, 2014).

Sassoon, Siegfried, *Memoirs of an Infantry Officer* (London: Faber, 1997).

Sebag-Montefiore, Hugh, *Somme: Into the Breach* (Cambridge, MA: Belknap, 2016).

Seldon, Anthony, and David Walsh, *Public Schools and the Great War* (Barnsley: Pen & Sword, 2013).

Sheldon, Jack, *The Germans at Beaumont Hamel* (Barnsley: Pen & Sword, 2006).

Winter, Jay, ed., *La Première Guerre Mondiale* (Paris: Fayard, 2014).

# ACKNOWLEDGEMENTS

I am not a professional historian and have fortunately benefited, as in my previous endeavour, from the invaluable support of my mentor, Stéphane Audoin-Rouzeau, who has proven so generous with his time and knowledge alike. I have also profited from the warm and comforting support of all of the young (and not so young) scholars, PhDs, PhD candidates and diverse enthusiasts who meet in the context of his various seminars at the École des Hautes Études en Sciences Sociales (EHESS). I of course owe an immense debt of gratitude to John Horne, a true eminence in the field of First World War studies, for kindly agreeing to supply the foreword to this work.

I would like to thank particularly the (relatively!) young scholars who have for years been the driving force behind the 'Poilu' seminar on the 'Historiography of the First World War'. I am especially grateful to Laurence Campa, Chloé Drieu, Victor Demiaux, Galit Haddad, Franziska Heimburger, Manon Pignot, Emmanuel Saint-Fuscien, Clémentine Vidal-Naquet and Arndt Weinrich for having tolerated me so long in their midst.

At Fayard, I once again had the privilege of working with Sophie Kucoyanis, a tireless, erudite, meticulous and friendly editor.

Finally, those who know me know to whom I owe my research and writing efforts.

It goes without saying that any errors, omissions or other imperfections are solely mine. For these, I beg the reader's indulgence.

# ENDNOTES

1   See the moving testimony of Stéphane Audoin-Rouzeau in Quelle histoire (Paris: Gallimard, 2013).

2   Jean-Michel Steg, *Death in the Ardennes: 22nd August 1914: France's Deadliest Day* (London: University of Buckingham Press, 2021). The original French edition is Jean-Michel Steg, *Le 22 août 1914: le jour le plus meurtrier de l'histoire de France* (Paris: Fayard, 2013).

3   In contrast to that of the main body of the army, which was intended to defend the national territory, the purpose of the Colonial Corps was to intervene everywhere overseas. It thus consisted of volunteers rather than conscripts.

4   The British only established conscription in early 1916. Some of its Dominions, such as Australia, never did so.

5   The Magna Carta dates from 1215.

6   Philippe Pétain, speech of 17 June 1941 on the occasion of the anniversary of the request for an armistice.

7   The 1st Essex, for its part, continued to advance as well as it could along the communication trenches and only joined the unsuccessful assault an hour later. This interval spared it many casualties.

8   Quoted in Martin Mace and John Grehan, *Slaughter on*

*the Somme: 1 July 1916: The Complete War Diaries of the British Army's Worst Day* (Barnsley: Pen & Sword, 2013).

9   And this despite the reluctance of Lord Kitchener, who wished to wait until 1917 in order to perfect the training of his volunteers and profit from advances in the British arms industry.

10   For convenience, I shall refer to the British army in France by the acronym BEF (British Expeditionary Force).

11   Quoted in William R. Griffiths, *The Great War* (1986; New York: Square One, 2003), p. 198.

12   In the absence of joint management of the conflict, the only example of large-scale Franco-British cooperation seems to be that of the Crimea campaign, which was conducted between 1853 and 1856 against the Russian Empire.

13   In mid-June 1916, Lord Kitchener died when the boat that was transporting him to Russia for the purpose of conversations with the imperial general staff was shipwrecked north of Scotland.

14   Olivier Cosson, *Préparer la Grande Guerre: l'armée française et la guerre russo-japonaise* (1899–1914) (Paris: Les Indes Savantes, 2013).

15   Named after the man who invented them in the course of the Napoleonic Wars, the British major Henry Shrapnel (1761–1842).

16   Melinite, for example.

17   The first British tank, the Mark 1, was developed by Colonel Ernest Swinton (1868–1951), a brilliant technician. He named it the tank (that is, reservoir) in order to conceal its purpose. General Jean Baptiste Eugène Estienne (1860–1936), for his part, developed the first French armoured vehicles, the Schneider and, later, Saint-Chamond tanks.

18   Fritz Haber (1868–1934) was one of the most brilliant scientists of his generation. Of Jewish origin but a fervent German nationalist, he converted to Protestantism. His wife, Clara Immerwahr, was also a renowned chemist and the first woman to receive a doctorate from the University of Breslau. In complete disagreement with her husband as to the manner in which he used his research during the war, she committed suicide following the first deployment of poison gas. In 1920, Fritz Haber received the Nobel Prize in Chemistry for the year

1918. The representatives of the Allied powers boycotted the award ceremony. In 1934, he was ejected from his chair at the University of Freiburg despite a personal appeal to Hitler by the renowned physicist Max Planck. Haber died in Basel while on route to exile in England, where he had (despite everything) been offered a post at Cambridge.

19    Quoted in Stephen Bull, *Trench: A History of Warfare on the Western Front* (Oxford: Osprey, 2010), p. 125.

20    'Greek fire', for example: jets of inflammable resin used by the Byzantine Empire.

21    ...which warmed until boiling, allowing one, it was claimed, to use the water to make tea.

22    The consequences of this bombardment were above all psychological. In all, nearly 300 shells fell on Paris, killing 256 people. The destructive effect of these enormous shells was limited since, in order to travel so far, their metal casing had to be very thick to prevent disintegration in flight. Similarly, a sufficient propulsive charge was required for the shell to travel over 100 kilometres, leaving room for only a few kilograms of useful explosive material. Finally, the barrels on these guns were rapidly worn out and required frequent reaming.

23    In fact, the Asquith government was eager to keep troops in Great Britain to deal with a potential civil war in Ireland. Fighting ultimately broke out at Easter 1916, though it remained relatively contained.

24    Given the need for men, in late 1915 the minimum height for enlistment in the army was reduced to 1.58 metres.

25    Representing around 20 per cent of the inter-Allied force.

26    The annual distribution of French military losses in the conflict (excepting those who went missing) is as follows:

> 1914 (five months): 300,000 (Battle of the Frontiers and Battle of the Marne)
> 1915: 340,000 (Battle of Artois and Battle of Champagne)
> 1916: 250,000 (Battle of Verdun and Battle of the Somme)
> 1917: 155,000 (Battle of Chemin des Dames)
> 1918: 240,000 (German offensive, followed by Allied offensive)

27    A sap is a mine gallery dug under an enemy position where explosives are placed and detonated in order to destroy it.

28    Raymond Poincaré, *Mémoires*, vol. vi (Paris: Plon, 1930), p. 276.

29    In the popular imagination, the mobilization of Parisian taxis to transport several thousand soldiers north-east of Paris more rapidly had assumed disproportionate significance relative to its real military impact.

30    In 1916, Army Group North consisted of the Sixth and Tenth armies. British and Belgian troops were also integrated into this system.

31    A French army corps consisted of two or three divisions, each possessing around 15,000 men. On the maps, the army corps are indicated with the abbreviation 'XXX', followed by the appropriate number, while divisions are indicated with the abbreviation 'XX'.

32    At this time, Germans leaders demanded the following drastic conditions in exchange for peace with France:
- France was to accept formally the annexation of Alsace and Lorraine by the Second Reich.
- France was to acquiesce to the further annexation of the iron- and steel-manufacturing basin around Briey.
- France was to agree to pay massive war reparations.

33    As would be the case of the German army in November 1918.

34    Thus the importance of protecting access roads to the front, particularly the famous 'Voie Sacrée' ('sacred way'), which allowed for the uninterrupted transport of troops between front and rear.

35    Especially given the incipient collapse of the Austro-Hungarian army.

36    The only two exceptions were the Newfoundland Regiment, which had been integrated into the British 29th Division, and a battalion of Bermudan soldiers. Both units experienced disastrous casualties in the course of the 1 July attack.

37    Quoted in Paul Kendall, *Somme 1916: Success and Failure on the First Day of the Battle of the Somme* (Barnsley: Frontline, 2015), p. 61.

38    Quoted in Martin Middlebrook, *The First Day on the Somme: 1 July 1916* (1971; London: Penguin, 2006), ch. 6.

39    Quoted in Alan Axelrod, *The Battle of the Somme* (Guilford, CT: Lyons Press, 2016), p. 155.

40    Quoted in Anne Duménil, 'La bataille de la Somme et

l'expérience de combat des soldats allemands de la Grande Guerre', in Philippe Nivet, ed., *La Bataille en Picardie* (Amiens: Encrage, 2000), pp. 113–14.

41   Ernst Jünger, *Storm of Steel*, trans. Michael Hofmann (London: Penguin, 2003).

42   A handful of sources speak of men escorted to the rear by military police with self-inflicted wounds to the hand, knee or foot. That said, one must in these conditions distinguish between panicked fear and the clumsiness induced by the extreme agitation of the hours preceding battle... and rum.

43   Available at https://cudl.lib.cam.ac.uk/view/MS-ADD-09852-00001-00007/21.

44   Cut down upon reaching the German barbed wire, Captain Nevill of the 30th Division did not win his bet to make it to the German trench with his football. One of his soldiers nevertheless won the prize and the victorious football is today on display at the regimental museum of the East Surreys.

45   A symbol of the influence of geography on history, this straight road was an ancient Roman route used to transport defenders rapidly to forts defending against Germanic invaders.

46   Against orders, the commander of the Glasgow Commercials Regiment had his men charge at the start of the attack, allowing them to conquer the enemy trench before most of the German defenders had had time to leave their shelters.

47   The Lochnagar crater is today one of the most visited sites on the Somme front.

48   This aspect of the plan was obviously not presented to the troops in question.

49   It must be noted that the British patriotism of these Irish Protestant soldiers was white-hot at the time. At Easter of that year, the long-brewing civil war in Ireland had broken out, with an uprising of Catholic nationalist groups in Dublin.

50   Quoted in William Philpott, *Bloody Victory* (London: Little, Brown, 2009), p. 191.

51   Martin Middlebrook, *The First Day on the Somme: 1 July 1916* (1971; London: Penguin, 2006).

52   Given the very homogeneous social origin of British officers, above all in this phase of the war, the British ruling classes

showed a notable willingness to accept the massive sacrifice of its members in certain specific circumstances such as these.

53    Quoted in Hugh Sebag-Montefiore, *Somme: Into the Breach* (Cambridge, MA: Belknap, 2016), pp. 101–2.

54    John Keegan, *The Face of Battle* (London: Penguin, 1978).

55    Over the course of their many colonial wars, British professional soldiers had a reputation for the effectiveness of their rifle fire. They had never had occasion to develop similar skills in heavy artillery.

56    As in France, however, many of them were gradually reassigned to their work benches.

57    Keegan, op. cit..

58    Quoted in Peter Hart, *The Great War: A Combat History of the First World War* (Oxford: Oxford University Press, 2013), p. 225.

59    In such episodes of accelerated technological change, the skills required by leaders are completely transformed. For example, fifty years ago, the most important position in the French media was doubtless that of the director of the now defunct daily *France Soir*... Today, it is hard to imagine anyone entrusting him with responsibility for managing Facebook.

60    Quoted in Jean-Yves Le Naour, *1916: l'enfer* (Paris: Perrin, 2014).

61    It was nevertheless torture for Joffre and subtle recompense for Haig. Since the king of England had sworn off alcohol for the duration of the war, none was served in the course of the meal. Joffre, who nearly choked when a waiter offered him lemonade, was obliged – doubtlessly a rare thing in what was a well-ordered existence in this domain – to remain sober throughout the lunch.

62    Fairness requires one to mention that, beginning in mid-1917 and continuing until the end of the conflict, the British high command did a noticeably better job of overseeing the fighting, particularly thanks to markedly improved performance on the part of the artillery.

63    Where, incidentally, the Newfoundland Regiment, now rebuilt with new volunteers who had arrived from Scotland, was once again sent into battle.

64  In this connection, see William Philpott's very interesting discussion of how casualties vary by source and the controversies surrounding this subject in *Bloody Victory* (London: Little, Brown, 2009), pp. 598–603. On the subject of the breakdown of British casualties, see also Robin Prior and Trevor Wilson, *The Somme* (New Haven, CT: Yale University Press, 2006).

65  See Anne Duménil, 'La bataille de la Somme et l'expérience de combat des soldats allemands de la Grande Guerre', in Philippe Nivet, ed., *La Bataille en Picardie* (Amiens: Encrage, 2000), p. 142.

66  Ibid., p. 149.

67  *Materialschlacht* was the term he gave this new phenomenon.

68  Asquith's wife, Margot, made the mistake of confiding to a journalist that she found her husband sobbing every night in their bedroom. See Anne de Courcy, *Margot at War* (London: Weidenfeld & Nicolson, 2014).

69  See Anthony Seldon and David Walsh, *Public Schools and the Great War* (Barnsley: Pen & Sword, 2013).

70  Though no more than it would take for the French to recognize the Battle of the Frontiers (August 1914) for the slaughter that it was. Even today, it is necessary to reiterate endlessly that, for the French army, the last ten days of August 1914 were the bloodiest period of the entire war.

71  Very rapidly and with some success, what's more... Credit for the French victory on the Marne in September 1914 may at least partly go to the pilot who identified the eastward bend in the path of the First Army (led by Alexander von Kluck), which thereby exposed the right flank of the German army to the French and British counter-offensive.

72  *The Battle of the Somme* [DVD] (London: Imperial War Museum, 2008).

73  *Bei unseren Helden an der Somme*, available for viewing at the Historial de Péronne.

74  Ministère des Armées, *Les Armées françaises dans la Grande Guerre*, vol. iv/2 (Paris: Imprimerie Nationale, 1933), p. 233.

75  Which in 1932 would provoke the first riots ever in the country's capital, St John's.

76  Written by John Oxenham, the pen name of the English poet William Arthur Dunkerley (1852–1941).